'This is a book on an important subject in a clear, accessible style. It will be pastorally helpful to a good number of people.'
The Rt Reverend Richard Harries,
Bishop of Oxford, 1987–2006

'An excellent and pastorally sympathetic treatment of a difficult subject, which I hope will be widely read.'
The Reverend Professor Keith Ward,
Regius Professor of Divinity, Oxford, 1991–2003

'This carefully argued book will be of real help to those troubled by the suggestion (I believe, mistaken) that the Christian God might exact unending suffering as the punishment for sins.'
The Reverend Dr John Polkinghorne, KBE, FRS,
former professor of Mathematical Physics, Cambridge

REVEREND DAVID CLAYTON pursued religious studies at the Methodist Cliff College in Derbyshire, and trained for the Baptist ministry at Spurgeons College, London. David served in both rural and urban pastorates retiring in January 2006 from the Pastorate. He continues his theological researches in eschatology. David is married and has two grown-up children.

'Hell' – Fact or Fiction?
Explorations in Human Destiny

David Clayton

ATHENA PRESS

LONDON

'Hell' – Fact or Fiction?
Explorations in Human Destiny
Copyright © David Clayton 2006

ISBN 1 84401 687 0

First Published 2006 by
ATHENA PRESS
Queen's House, 2 Holly Road
Twickenham TW1 4EG
United Kingdom

Printed for Athena Press

I wish to thank my publishers for their patient and careful editing, help and advice during the publication process, and a special word of thanks for Helen Orr who translated my handwritten work into readable computerised script. And of course thanks to my wife who exercised (and still does) patience and understanding with my preoccupation with human destiny, and to my children who have listened to me sounding off on the subject!

I would like to express my gratitude to Professor Keith Ward, the Reverend Dr Sir John Polkinghorne, and the one-time Bishop of Oxford Rt Reverend Richard Harries for kindly agreeing to read drafts of my work and in encouraging me to continue with my project.

I wish to express my thanks to the following, or/and their publishers, for granting their permission to use copyrighted material: Sheila Cassidy, Larry Dixon, David Edwards, Martin Israel, Bruce Milne, Chris Morgan, Jurgen Moltmann, John Polkinghorn, Nigel Wright, and the Evangelical Alliance.

To any copyright holders that I have not contacted, not been able to contact, unable to trace, the Author and Publisher would be pleased to be contacted so that in any future editions of this book acknowledgement can be made.

Lastly, I wish to thank the libraries of St Deiniol's in North Wales, the Society of Mary and Martha in Devon, Spurgeon's College in London, and Dr Williams in London for the use of their facilities.

I dedicate this book to all those who have helped and encouraged me in my spiritual journey, and who still do.

'Hell' – Fact or Fiction?
Explorations in Human Destiny

Contents

Introduction

In the year 2000, The Evangelical Alliance brought out a report on the nature of hell, where it stated:

> The 1980s and 1990s have seen evangelical biblical scholars and systematic theologians publish an unprecedented flow of material on hell, but the reality is that most Christians are led to deal with it through their everyday contact with unbelievers, through the death of non-Christian relatives, of friends, through participation in outreach projects, and through the queries of inquisitive children. We are also aware that many pastors, preachers and evangelists struggle to communicate this most difficult of topics in an accessible way. As members of a theological commission representing individuals, local churches and Christian agencies, we believe that it is important to address these practical concerns.[1]

After informing us that there is no room for evangelical smugness, after citing as an example of evangelical compassion Frances Schaeffer, who, when asked for a theological exposition of the nature of hell, instead remained silent and wept, the report goes on to discuss bringing people into the Kingdom of Heaven through fear, with one example after another from the mission history of the world. These include loving, compassionate individuals such as Hudson Taylor, founder of what was known as 'the China-inland Mission', who agonised over millions of Chinese who were without the consolations of the Gospel: '360 million Chinese souls dying?' William Booth maintained that if only his Salvation Army officers could spend one night in hell, the power of their mission would be immeasurably strengthened. And in our own time, John Blanchard is quoted:

> How can you possibly accept that multitudes of people, including

---

[1] 'The Nature of Hell', pp. 111–112.

many you know personally, are on a collision course with an announcement of righteous and terrifying condemnation, and yet do nothing to warn them of danger?[2]

David Pawson even goes as far as to say, 'to neglect to do this is to be in danger of eternal hell oneself!' This radically bad news goes on and on.

This doctrine of everlasting punishment, even annihilation, seriously handicaps evangelism. For all those brought to faith through conservative evangelical missions, vast numbers are prevented from doing so because of this understanding of the nature of hell; for some, it even means turning their backs on the Gospel.

I believe this concept of hell is also a handicap to worship. How can you lovingly and joyfully worship a God whom you know is, according to some conservative evangelical teaching, going to torture endlessly in the afterlife some of your dearest friends and relatives, if they do not make a decision for now? And it is of no great comfort to say, 'But we don't know if this will happen to them, for who knows what may take place in those last moments of transition from this world to the next?' It is surely enough to know that, according to this doctrine of hell, there is such a place of torment, and their souls suffer everlastingly in it; it is enough to know it is, according to this 'Nature of Hell', on the Creator's agenda!

What of people who cannot believe because of their own suffering, or that of their loved ones, or the world's? How would we react to someone who because a certain person wronged them, say twenty years ago, had ever since had them constantly punished, tortured every day, without let-up day and night, and still intended to treat them thus, till the end of their days in constant pain of body, mind and spirit?

I would suggest that the wonderful response to a number of evangelical missions is because the love of Christ is emphasised, not the fear of everlasting punishment in hell. This love is what is foundational to the proclamation of the good news. This is the

---

[2] Ibid.

love we are called to learn and live. This is the love from which true righteousness springs, and the kingdom of heaven on earth is realised.

The implications of the conclusions of the Evangelical Alliance's report, though produced by loving compassionate believers who long to see people coming to salvation, nevertheless builds a wall which bars many from entering that salvation. It builds a wall, which seen in all its stark conclusions prevents many from worship, mission and discipleship. Many cannot, try as they might, accept this 'Nature of Hell'.

It was reading the Evangelical Alliance Report that prompted me to write on this subject; to sensitive Christian souls, this doctrine has caused great pain; they have worried over the fate of loved ones, for whom there appears to be no hope unless they accept Christ as Saviour. The teaching on hell that is still taught by some ministers and theologians and is accepted by a number of churches today heightens the problem of suffering.

Some would accept the fact that there can be 'hell on earth', suffering of such intensity that 'it's sheer hell'; this for most people in the modern world is their understanding of the term 'hell'. To go beyond that, for many people, is to enter the world of fantasy. What is true, of course, is that while few people speculate and agonise over the question of hell, many more do speculate and agonise over the question of suffering. Is there ever going to be an end to personal and worldwide suffering? A belief in the nature of hell as everlasting punishment heightens the problem of suffering, and an alternative view of annihilation leaves one with questions of meaning and purpose.

Suffering has always been one of the barriers to belief, perhaps even the main one. With this in mind, my opening chapter looks at the question of suffering in relation to human destiny. I shall also consider in Chapter 1 how, for some, meaning is brought out of suffering, when love and compassion are infused into it, even bringing salvation to those afflicted by it, and those who are witnesses of it. Love released in the midst of hate, bitterness and extreme suffering from the cross of Christ brought forth meaning from apparent meaninglessness, resulting in salvation – the triumph of love over hate.

In the second chapter we shall see where Christ's emphasis lay during his earthly ministry in response to the assertion that Christ taught more about hell and judgement than anyone else in scripture. Chapter three looks at the actual word 'hell', its history and meaning; then in Chapter four we consider tradition and scripture. Chapter five looks at the ethos of scripture, what is its overall thrust, where its emphasis lies. Chapters six and seven search the scriptures of the Old and New Testaments with regard to judgement, everlasting punishment and destruction. This section also looks at the meaning of 'eternal'. Chapter Eight considers the teaching of the 'intermediate state', opportunity beyond this present earthly state for repentance and salvation. The final chapter looks at the foundation for salvation, in which I question the emphasis of what is implied in the term 'Justification by Faith'.

Over the years I have struggled with the concept of eternal punishment and annihilation. I have read and listened to conservative evangelical interpretations of scripture from those who write and speak out of a real love and desire to bring people into the Kingdom of God. But these expositions have not convinced me. I have therefore been moved to consider the views of those who hold to what has been described as a 'wider hope'.

I have also been prompted to write on this subject by what has emerged in my pastoral work. I believe in grass-roots theology that endeavours to respond to pastoral needs. Christ's own theology, it seems to me, was worked out in the nitty-gritty of life, not in fantasy. He dealt with what were real issues for people he came in contact with. From aspects of life he pointed to aspects of Heaven, dealing with suffering, emotional, mental and, not the least, spiritual.

In order to try and understand human destiny, in particular the teaching on hell, I have found it necessary to paddle in the pool of the academics. I am indebted to a number of scholars, including F W Farrar, especially appreciating his expertise in the original languages of Holy Scripture, and Jan Bonda for a twentieth century in-depth study resulting in a biblically based conclusion, which highlights the ultimate mercy of God in the salvation of mankind. Both these men have been prompted to write out of their pastoral experience, one from the late nineteenth century, the other from the late twentieth. Other scholars I am indebted to I have acknowledge within the text, together with the sources, whenever possible, and in the Bibliography. Thomas Allin has also been a great help in my chapters 'Searching the Scriptures' and for his .contribution to the 'wider hope' in eschatology.

It may be looked upon as rather presumptuous on my part to write on this subject when I am not a professional theologian and not an academic, but as stated, this work is prompted by pastoral considerations. Much has been written by scholars for which I am sincerely grateful, but I believe there is room for a non-academic pastor's pen, who can no longer hold back from putting his thoughts down on paper.

In its introduction, the Evangelical Alliance Report states the question that all ask at some point in their lives:

> 'What happens when we die?' This is one of the great questions of life. It has prompted diverse responses from philosophers, artists, scientists and religious leaders. In the Christian context, however, it has most typically been answered in terms of a decisive contrast – the contrast between Heaven and hell.[3]

And this is just the point. The contrast is seen in Heaven being eternal, everlasting and hell being terminal; that wrongdoing in thought, word and deed will be no more, whereas healthy, beautiful, exciting, wonderful miraculous love will, in all its mercy, grace and vitality, never end. For those seriously thinking about the Christian faith, who are attracted by the witness of good Christians down the ages, and who are sincerely thinking of discovering a meaning to life and who think that the Christian faith could well supply the answer, and who have loving bonds with dear relatives and friends who have died and want to know if there is something beyond (especially if those dear ones have not, to their knowledge, made any confession of faith), then the doctrine of hell as expounded by some Christians, and as put forth in the E A Report,

---

[3] Introduction, 'The Nature of Hell', p.1.

will be, and has been, a real stumbling block to their acceptance of the Christian Gospel.

The nature of hell has of course been debated by academics throughout history. The three basic positions are: annihilation at the final judgement after a period of punishment for sins, everlasting punishment or universal salvation.

Some have criticised universal salvation on the grounds that it offers cheap grace.

Sir John Polkinghorne draws attention to the dying poet Heine:

> When asked if he were concerned about the consequences of his dissolute life, he said, 'God will pardon me. That is his line of business!' On the other hand, if we were certain that there are some who will be in hell forever, we might ask why it was that God allowed them to be part of the divine creation at all. Not all our perplexities can be resolved in this life.[4]

It must be observed however that universal salvation does not exclude a period of remedial punishment. It is also true that we read in 1 Corinthians 13: 12–13:

> We don't yet see things clearly. We're squinting in a fog, peering through a mist. But it won't be long before the weather clears and the sun shines bright! We'll see it all then, see it all as clearly as God sees us, knowing him directly just as he knows us!…[5]
>
> There are three things that last for ever: Faith, hope and love; but the greatest of them all is love.'[6]

I do believe that an understanding of life beyond the dissolution of the body, however 'misty', can enable one to live more fully in the present, living with and through the handicaps of life, spiritual and physical, and to appreciate life on a vaster scale, especially when the 'wider hope' of eternal destiny is considered.

---

[4] *The God of Hope and the End of the World*, S P C K, 2002, pp.137–138.

5 E Peterson's translation, 'The Message', Navpress, 1995.

[6] *The New English Bible*, Oxford University Press, 1970.

Chapter 1: Introducing Hell – Suffering

A young man is sweating it out in prayer, kneeling at his bedside. He is praying for his parents, he is praying for their salvation. Fear grips him, for his parents have not 'accepted Christ'. They have not made a 'commitment', and according to what this young man has been taught, that must mean they are doomed to everlasting punishment in hell or annihilation. But his parents have committed no great crime, they have tried to live good lives; yet this will not save them.

There is a widely accepted teaching among some Christians which, put simply, states that unless a person has accepted Christ as Saviour, however good they may be, they will go to hell, whereas one who has will go to heaven. The alternative for some is annihilation after punishment beyond the grave.[7] There is something very wrong here in understanding what it means to 'accept Christ'. It is also crucial to understand what the Bible means when it states, in various ways, that it is only through Christ that one is saved – we shall look at the biblical evidence later.

Here is a man who is having to work through a bereavement for a much loved wife, who on top of this, has to handle the fact that one of his children, his daughter, no longer gets anything from the church service she now attends – but who goes to support her father. A young woman, loving and supportive, of a kind and generous nature.

---

[7] Known as 'conditional immortality', a person's immortality depends on their acceptance of Christ as Saviour now, in this mortal life. Without this acceptance, there will be extinction at death, or according to some, after a period of punishment for sins committed. When 'conditional immortality' includes a period of punishment before extinction, it seems to have no more meaning or purpose than everlasting punishment, to suffer and then to be annihilated has no remedial benefit. When we look at the Old Testament, it does appear that all punishment was intended to turn Israel back to righteousness; it had a purpose, it was remedial, its purpose being the ultimate saving of Israel.

The father has to cope with the fact that his dear wife, before she died, said the most difficult thing to bear was that she would not see her daughter anymore because she no longer professed the faith she had been brought up in – a difficult thought for her father to handle, to put it mildly.

Here is another person, a loving father and husband dying of a very painful cancer – a non-believer, with a very close relationship with his wife and family, who said what he was most concerned about was the trouble he was causing his family; during this time there were some very pressing questions about his illness, pain and eternal destiny, from his loved ones.[8]

There are loving and sincere people who pour out their lives for others in love and care, but cannot believe in God. Why? Because of all the suffering they have seen in the world. This is not a 'red herring', it is a genuine difficulty, a genuine barrier to belief. They want to believe but can't.

Or take a person in a concentration camp. A believer in the God of his fathers, an Orthodox Jew, but one who no longer believes because of his own suffering and the suffering of those around him. Does the Christian faith condemn such a person to be taken from a living hell on earth to a never-ending torment in a hell beyond the grave?

Sheila Cassidy, in her book *Good Friday People* draws attention to Elie Wiesel's book *Night*, and writes:

> ...Wiesel captures the deepest theological reality:
> 'Where is God? Where is He? Someone behind me asked ...Where is God now? And I heard a voice within me answer him: Where is He? Here He is – He is hanging here on this gallows.' ...
>
> For Elie Wiesel, a deeply religious Jewish boy of fourteen reared on the Talmud and longing to be initiated into the mystical writings of the cabbala, both God and his faith died in Auschwitz.
>
> 'Never shall I forget that night, the first night in the camp, which has turned my life into one long night, seven times cursed and seven times sealed. Never shall I forget that smoke. Never shall I forget the little faces of the children whose bodies I saw

---

[8] These are real circumstances coming from experiences during my own pastoral ministry.

turned into wreaths of smoke beneath a silent blue sky. Never shall I forget those flames which consumed my faith forever. Never shall I forget that nocturnal silence which deprived me, for all eternity, of the desire to live. Never shall I forget those moments which murdered my God and my soul and turned my dreams to dust. Never shall I forget these things, even if I am condemned to live as long as God Himself. Never.'

François Mauriac, who met Wiesel, described him as having the look of…a Lazarus risen from the dead, yet still a prisoner within the grim confines where he had stayed, stumbling among the shameful corpses. [9]

'Rich in faith himself, Mauriac could find no words to release the young man from his prison.

'And I, who believe that God is Love, what answer could I give my young questioner, whose dark eyes still held the reflection of that angelic sadness which had appeared one day upon the face of the hanged child? What did I say to him? Did I speak of that other Israeli, his brother, who may have resembled him – the Crucified, whose Cross has conquered the world? Did I affirm that the stumbling block to his faith was the cornerstone of mine, and that the conformity between the Cross and the suffering of men was in my eyes the key to that impenetrable mystery whereon the faith of his childhood had perished? Zion, however, has risen up again from the crematories and the charnel houses. The Jewish nation has been resurrected from among its thousands of dead. It is through them that it lives again. We do not know the worth of one single drop of blood, one single tear. All is grace. If the Eternal is the Eternal, the last word for each one of us belongs to Him. This is what I should have told this Jewish child. But I could only embrace him, weeping.'

I'm sure Mauriac knew deep in his heart, as I know from my experience of accompanying the suffering, that his tears were worth more than a thousand theological explanations. And yet, as thinking, rational human beings we must always struggle to make sense of the dual realities of our life as Christians: the existence of appalling wickedness and suffering, and our belief in a loving God. Each time I get drawn into this search I find myself caught up in the mystery and paradox of the Scriptures, particularly the Fourth Song of the Servant, Isaiah, Chapter 53.

---

[9] François Mauriac, in the introduction to Night by Elie Wiesel.

'Who could believe what we have heard,
and to whom has the power of Yahweh been revealed?'
Like a sapling he grew up in front of us,
like a root in arid ground.
Without beauty, without majesty (we saw him),
no looks to attract our eyes:
a thing despised and rejected by men,
a man of sorrows and familiar with suffering,
a man to make people screen their faces;
he was despised and we took no account of him.
And yet ours were the sufferings he bore,
ours the sufferings he carried.
But we, we thought of him as someone punished,
struck by God, and brought low.
Yet he was pierced through for our faults,
crushed for our sins.
On him lies a punishment that brings us peace,
and through his wounds we are healed.

It is this passage, I think, more than any other, that has brought me to where I now stand in my understanding of the mystery of suffering, for I see in the 'man of sorrows' the face not only of Jesus but of all my Good Friday people. There are the people who make us want to screen our faces, to turn away, and yet it is through them that the grace of God flows to water our arid souls. These people are the hollowed bamboo through which the life-giving water flows, the reed pipes on which the musician plays his song.10

There have been those in concentration camps who, in spite of their own and other people's suffering, have, none the less, possessed a faith of such quality that it has been a source of strength to those around them as well as themselves. They have not only held fast to a belief in a loving God and Saviour, they have expressed his love in the most excruciating circumstances and given hope to the dying now and for ever.

---

[10] Sheila Cassidy, *Good Friday People*, Darton, Longman and Todd, 1991, pp3–5. Sheila Cassidy was a Palliative care physician at Plymouth General Hospital, she made headlines in 1975 when she was arrested and tortured in Chile for treating a revolutionary, a story she recounts in her book *Audacity to Believe*.

In Auschwitz, where hunger and hatred reigned, and faith evaporated, Maximilian Kolbe opened his heart to others and spoke of God's infinite love. He never seemed to think of himself. When food was brought in, and everyone struggled to get a place in the queue to be sure of his share, Maximilian stood aside, so that frequently there was none for him. At other times he shared his meagre ration of soup or bread with others. He once told another priest, 'We must be grateful we are here. There is so much for us to do; look how people need us.'[11]

Finally he took the place of another in the death block and ministered hope and comfort even there, bringing in worship and prayer in place of despair.

Another light in the darkness was Maria Skobtsova in Ravensbruck concentration camp.

Her robust constitution, wide ranging interests and habit of prayer saved her from being utterly disoriented by the conditions prevailing in Ravensbruck. Others were not so fortunate. There, in the camp, human misery and suffering were taken to breaking point. At three each morning the women had to stand out in the open in all weathers, until everyone had been counted, a procedure (known as the appel) that regularly took five or more hours. Maria took it calmly; many could not. Maria would not succumb to despair. 'Whatever you do,' she begged them, 'continue to think. Don't allow the flame of your spirit to die. In conflict with doubt, cast your thoughts wider and deeper. Do not let your thoughts be debased. Let it transcend the conditions and limitations of this earth.'

To illustrate her meaning, she pointed to the camps three crematoria whose chimneys continuously belched out smoke, a constant reminder of the nearness to death.

'It is only here, immediately above the chimneys, that the smoke is oppressive,' explained Maria. 'When it rises higher, it turns into light clouds before being dispersed into limitless space. In the same way our souls, once they have torn themselves away from this sinful earth, move by means of an effortless unearthly flight into eternity, where there's life full of joy.'[12]

---

[11] From *Saints of the Twentieth Century*, Brother Kenneth, CGA, Mowbrays, 1976, pp. 97–98.
[12] *Candles in the Dark*, Mary Craig, (Spire) Hodder & Stoughton, 1984, p. 240–241.

'She had a special place for the young women communist soldiers,' we read, 'she took them under her wing.' A survivor said, 'We were cut off from our families; yet somehow she provided us with a family.'

> Maria was mother to them all, but particularly to the young Soviet women soldiers in Block 31 whom she adopted as her own, hugging them like children when they were afraid,.... It was essential to the Nazi philosophy to degrade and brutalise the human spirit before destroying the body. Maria fought back. On Easter Day 1944 she decorated the windows of her barracks with astonishing beautiful paper cut-outs (she used paper stolen from the Germans) ...the other prisoners turned to her for comfort.[13]

We notice that she held out eternal hope for all, for Soviet young women soldiers, who, coming from an atheist state, presumably held no belief in God. In fact, she had a special place in her heart for them. We notice that Bonhoeffer would not take a service for inmates of his prison while a devout communist was excluded. They had gone through so much together as a group, and he did not want any to feel left out. It was not until the man himself came to Bonhoeffer (without any pressure) asking to be included, that he agreed to take the service.

Bonhoeffer preached from Isaiah 53:5, Peter's Epistle and John's Gospel.

Payne Best remembers: 'He reached the hearts of us all. Finding just the right words to express the spirit of our imprisonment and the thoughts and resolutions which it brought.' (While the men were reflecting on his words, he was taken away to be executed) '...leaving a whispered message for Payne Best for his old friend Bishop Bell, "Tell him," he said, "that for me this is the end, but also the beginning."'[14]

---

[13] Ibid.

[14] Ibid. p. 54. Bonhoeffer in Tegel Prison in 1944 in his work, *Last of the stations on the road to freedom*, wrote on death, 'Come now, thou greatest of feasts on the journey to freedom eternal; death, cast aside all the burdensome chains, and demolish the walls of our temporal body, the walls of our souls that are blinded, so that at last we may see that which remains hidden. Freedom, how long have we

Why do I give these examples, apart from showing that some, even in the most horrific circumstances, were lights in the darkness? I give these because they ministered to those whose faith had burnt low or was snuffed out due to the horrors that surrounded them. But what of those who did not have a Maria Skobtsova, a Maximilian Kolbe or a Bonhoeffer to lift them up, who died in pain and despair, who did not believe in anything anymore, God or man? Were they then, as we have already noted, to be taken from despair here to eternal despair beyond the grave, because they could no longer believe in anything? Did not Christ himself have a special word of peace to those disciples who had lost faith and hope after the crucifixion? For, in spite of all the teaching they had received from Christ over the past three years, when they saw him dead on a cross, they believed it was all over. In the face of the torture and death of one they loved, and had pinned all their hopes on, they could not believe. Numbed, they huddled together in an upper room, unable to think, to act, because of the pain and suffering they had seen.

Even when the women came to them with the news that Christ had risen, they still could not believe what they were told; all their senses told them it was the end.

'They regarded it as idle tales,' as the Authorised Version puts it, or as the New International Version has it, 'But they did not believe the women, because their words seemed to them like nonsense.' (Luke 24:11) But the Lord Jesus then appears to them himself; there is not one word of rebuke to these hurt faithless disciples, there is only the wonderful words – 'Peace be with you!' And he repeats his words of peace to them after showing them his hands and his side. Yes, he was the same Jesus of Nazareth, with the marks of his suffering still on him, but he is resurrected! Not a ghost. He is their same dear Jesus, come back from the dead, to assure, comfort, and encourage them, and give them a commission to tell the world the good news. Jesus understands loss of faith due to suffering in this world, and his love is greater than our doubts. His belief in us greater than our disbelief in him.

---

sought thee in discipline, action and suffering; dying, we now may behold thee revealed in the Lord.'

It is good to know that there are those who in spite of all kinds of handicaps and questions about life, its problems and pains, believe in and express the love of God. It must also be acknowledged that with the best will in the world there are those that can't.

We must also recognise that there are Christians of deep compassion who believe in everlasting punishment for the unrepentant in this life, or annihilation after a period of punishment; that the only opportunity to change, to respond to Christ, is in this present earthly life, with no hope of responding beyond the grave.

It must also be noted that increasing numbers of Christians do not accept the teaching of eternal punishment or punishment followed by extinction.[15]

David Edwards reminds us that even in the nineteenth century this was being expressed, and quotes the famous Victorian Prime Minister, Gladstone, who said, 'The traditional idea of hell has been banished to the far corners of the Christian mind.'

However, as David Edwards observes, 'It seems to be more accurate now than it was when he made it.'[16] For in the nineteenth century there were strong advocates of eternal punishment, such as the famous Victorian Baptist preacher, C H Spurgeon, a compassionate man who, among other achievements, founded an orphanage and a college, but who with his strong Calvinist theology could in his preaching paint lurid pictures of hell. For example, in his sermon, 'On the resurrection of the dead', with reference to those destined for hell, he proclaims:

> When thou diest thy soul will be tormented alone; that will be a hell for it. But at the day of judgement thy body will join thy soul, and then thou wilt have twin-hells, thy soul sweating drops of blood, and thy body suffused with agony. In the fire exactly like that which we have on earth thy body will lie, asbestos-like, for-

---

[15] Known as 'conditional immortality' – see footnote 7.

[16] *After Death?*, David Edwards, p.135. Edwards comments that the change here is of very great importance, for during most of its history the Christian mind has been filled again and again with graphic pictures of the torture chamber in which most men, women and children suffer and scream forever. It is also true, one must add, that there have always been those who have rejected this.

ever unconsumed, all thy veins roads for the feet of pain to travel on, every nerve a string on which the Devil shall forever play his diabolical tune of hell's unutterable lament![17]

It must be noted that C H Spurgeon had a great love for humanity and preached and wrote a great deal concerning the love of Christ. It is sad that in regard to Hell, he felt compelled to accept the doctrine of eternal punishment and for, indeed, love for humanity, give warnings of this doctrine in such terms. On the other hand in 1877, you had F W Farrar, Dean of Canterbury, Rector of St Margaret's Westminster, and maternal grandfather of Field Marshal Montgomery, who got into deep water for preaching a series of sermons which were eventually published under the title 'Eternal Hope'. It was these sermons and this book that brought him much criticism, as well as responses of deepest gratitude.

In Victorian England the question of eternal destiny was a very hot potato indeed; it became even hotter when the Rector of St Margaret's, Westminster, in the winter of 1877, during the ordinary course of his residence as a Canon, preached a sermon from 1 Peter 4:6. It was not preached with publication in mind, it was preached out of a pastoral heart. It was preached by a man with a vast knowledge of scripture, with the original languages of the Bible at his fingertips; it was preached by a man who came to his subject not merely from an academic standpoint, but from a man who was very much in the world but not of it. A man who proclaimed the Gospel of eternal hope passionately, because in this world he had experienced at first-hand the hopelessness that surrounded those whose knowledge of Christ excluded the hope of Christ. Whose knowledge of the Gospel gave them no assurance because of a deficient understanding of scripture as sadly proclaimed by some of the most famous teachers of the day – teachers who had, it seems, failed to grasp the vastness of the Gospel of eternal hope, and in so doing had conveyed to thousands a Gospel of limited hope, or a Gospel of no hope.

I had become aware that the minds of many of the living were hopelessly harassed and – I can use no other word – devastated by

---

[17] *Mercy and Judgement*, quoted by F W Farrar, p. 104, MacMillan & Co, 1881.

the horror with which they brooded over the fate of the dead. The happiness of their lives shattered, the peace of their souls destroyed, not by the source of earthly bereavement, but by the terrible belief that brother or son, or wife, or husband had passed away into physical anguish and physical torment, endless beyond all utterance – excruciating. Such thoughts did not trouble the careless and brutal, who might be supposed to need them, they troubled only the tender-hearted and sincere. They were the direct result of the religious teaching they had received from their earliest years. To the irreligious poor, the common presentment of endless torment was a mere stumbling block; to the best of the religious it was a permanent misery. The irreligious are driven to disbelieve in any punishment because they have heard the punishment with which they are threatened described in such a way as to be utterly unbelievable. The religious accept these coarse pictures, and are either hardened by them into lovelessness or crushed into despair. Pharisaism and infidelity are the twin children of every form of theology, which obscures the tenderness of revelation, and belies the love of God.[18]

Although the above was written in the late 1800s, it still has relevance today. If one were to ask an orthodox evangelical (or what is generally recognised as being evangelical and orthodox) how they feel about the thought that, according to the tradition they hold, a dear brother or sister, mother, father or some close relative or friend, if they do not accept Christ before death, are doomed to eternal pain of mind, body and spirit, with never any chance of relief – and this for someone who has committed no recognisably horrific sin and has even tried to do the best they can, to help others in life – I suggest they would, if they think about this belief at all, be plunged into that condition that F W Farrar refers to above 'crushed in despair'. And I would make the observation that it would be the same today, as in Farrar's day, that if you were to expound this doctrine of eternal punishment to the irreligious, they would be driven to disbelief in any such punishment as 'utterly unbelievable'.

On the evening of 18th February 1998, Anthony Flew and William Lane Craig debated the question, 'Does God exist?' Some four thousand university students and faculty of Wisconsin

---

[18] Ibid. pp. 5–6.

University attended. Although the debate was on the question 'Does God exist?' the question of eternal punishment in hell was constantly coming up. Dr Flew, concluding his opening statement, brings up the question of eternal punishment to which he will return again and again; he stated:

'...apparently the God whom Dr Craig is asking us to believe is the creator, very much wants people to believe in a certain way and he wants this so much that he's prepared to torture them forever to punish them for not obeying "Me". Well, it seems to me that anyone who knew that this was what this cosmic "Saddam Hussein" wanted would behave like the sensible subjects of Saddam Hussein. They would say anything about his merits and goodness. Wouldn't you, if you were going to fall into the hands of his torturers? But omnipotence could avoid all this by simply making them such that they would choose to obey him...'

Craig's answer was – it is logically impossible to make someone freely do something. God's omnipotence does not mean that he can do things that are logically impossible.

Craig points out in his rebuttal of Flew's arguments that the existence or non-existence of hell is not the question under debate; but as one who believes in hell he feels he must respond. One of the points he makes in response is as follows:

'...if a person committed an infinite number of sins, then he would deserve eternal punishment. Now obviously no one commits an infinite number of sins in this life, but what about in the afterlife? In so far as the damned in hell continue to hate and reject God, they continue to sin, and thus they incur further punishment. And thus, in a real sense, hell is self-perpetuating; because the sinning goes on forever, the punishment goes on forever. Finally, I want to suggest that there may be in fact a sin of infinite gravity and proportion which does merit eternal punishment, and this would be the sin of irrevocably rejecting God and His forgiveness. It seems to me that for the creature to spit in the face of God, his creator – to reject God irrevocably – is a sin of infinite proportion and could merit eternal punishment.'

(Anthony Flew and William Lane Craig debate – 'Does God Exist',

p. 28, Ashgate, edited by Stan W Wallace, 2003. Since writing this, it has been reported that Anthony Flew has come to a theistic view of the universe.)

What is missing, it seems to me, in this debate is what I regard as the only answer possible, an answer found in many religions and none. That is the element of compassionate benevolent love, what the New Testament calls agape love. This love will woo and go on wooing until love breaks down resistance, not by force, but by being what it is, love. This is surely what Jesus Christ did on the cross when he cried out, 'Father, forgive them, they know not what they do.' As far as his executioners were concerned, they did know what they were doing; but Jesus knew better and even without their repentance at this time he is calling out for their forgiveness.

As regards Craig's suggestion of an infinite sin, surely the whole point of agape love is that love defeats evil. If people are forever sinning in eternity, surely this means that sin, wrong-doing, wrong attitudes, are not defeated. Jesus on the cross defeated evil not by wanting punishment for punishment, but the opposite, crying out for mercy on those who were punishing him – their forgiveness. This love is grace. Grace is giving to the undeserving what they do not deserve.

Later on we shall look more closely at this whole concept of saving love, with regard to just punishment, saving love as the foundation of salvation.

It is very noticeable that this debate could not avoid the subject of everlasting punishment; it is closely related to suffering in our world, and thus closely related to the creator. Thus the first chapter on this subject is to do with suffering.

The Dutch Reformed Pastor, Jan Bonda, has done a detailed study of this subject in his book *The One Purpose of God*.[19] It has been described as 'probably the most detailed study to have emerged from this marginal strand of evangelical universalism in recent times'.[20] He writes from his pastoral experience as follows:

---

[19] *The One Purpose of God* (an answer to the doctrine of eternal punishment) 1993 (Uitqeverij Ten Have b.v., Baarn). English edition, 1998, W B Eerdmans.
[20] 'The Nature of Hell', a report by the Evangelical Alliance Commission on unity and truth among Evangelicals (ACUTE), p. 32, 2000.

Throughout my life the gloomy doctrine of eternal punishment, which the church has preached for many centuries, has bothered me. After my retirement from the active ministry I at last had the opportunity to make an in-depth study of what the Bible has to say about this topic. I knew that many others had written about this subject, and I took the time to read their writings. What they wrote about the hope of salvation for all again and again strengthened my convictions. I decided, however, to take a different approach – a more systematic, biblical study that would also deal with the 'difficult texts' that are invariably cited against the hope of salvation for the millions. That is what I have done in this book, and in such a way that it can be read even by those without formal theological training.[21]

We note that Bonda and Farrar's theology is 'pastoral'; it is developed and worked out in the experiences of life – all theology needs to be rooted here. The question of eternal destiny raises the issue of meaning for humanity.

There are a number of unfinished arguments going on about the nature and value of human beings. Some of us keep asking questions about souls and people, the material and the spiritual, identity, death and resurrection. It still seems both possible and important to try to find out about what used to be called 'the end of man', whether it still makes sense – and if so, what sense – to affirm that we are made in God's image.[22]

Whereas hell may be regarded as irrelevant to life in the modern world, human destiny is relevant in individual and cosmic terms – it relates directly to how we view our daily lives, and the life of humanity as a whole; and this will have direct relevance as to how we treat each other, and how we relate to nature.

Our view of ourselves has ethical implications, this is self-evident. And so we direct our attention to the relevance of suffering in regard to the doctrine of hell. It is clear that in order to have an understanding of our relationship to our creator we must look at the kind of creator we are thinking of.

---

[21] From the Preface, p.xxiv, *The One Purpose of God.*
[22] *The Hope of Heaven,* Helen Oppenheimer, Cowley Publications, usp, p. 13.

To have a view of a creator that intends to torture forever those who oppose him, or to annihilate them, is to have a view of humanity that encourages the same! If we are made in the image of God, and if this God goes in for torture, then it follows in certain circumstances that it's okay for his creatures to do it!

Torture is surely the work of evil, the Devil, rather than the creator. Jesus Christ is the embodiment of love and compassion, creative rather than destructive.

The doctrines of evil, the Devil, eternal punishment, cause unending suffering throughout history.

> In the mid-Eighties, the world saw an odd and symbolic case of geographical transference. The President of the United States, Ronald Reagan, called the USSR, 'The Evil Empire', while the de facto leader of Iran, the Ayatollah Khomeini, called the United States, 'The Great Satan'. Both flights of rhetoric indicate that hell, the kingdom of the Devil, doesn't appear to be situated in the same place for everybody, and that the Devil is a politically useful figure.
>
> In 1992 Ali Benhadi, the chief aide to the leader of the Islamic Front for Algerian Salvation, ascribed a political role to the Devil by declaring that 'any party that strays from the precepts of God, the Koran, and the Sunnites is the Devil's party.' Benhadi was relegating the near totality of the planet's political parties to hell...
>
> In other words, if God cannot exist in a democracy, then the Devil, the creator's enemy, cannot either – and yet, a secular society is a society that belongs to the Devil. Such pronouncements should elicit neither ready outcries nor easy jeers. Through its secular arms, Christianity governed since its early triumph according to the principle of the Devil's existence and presence in all things that threaten the mutual will of the Pope and Potentate. Tens of thousands of lives have been sacrificed to this theocratic conception of State.[23]

First, it is as well that Massadie gives us some background as to where he is coming from, a bad Catholic education. There is however good Catholic education i.e. great Christian saints such as Maximillian Kolbe, Mother Teresa, and so on. Secondly, not all

---

[23] *The History of the Devil*, Gerald Massadie, 1996, Newleaf, an inprint of Boxtree Ltd, pp. 3–4.

Christians have used the weapons of the Devil; there has always been the genuine article as well as counterfeit Christianity, as with most things. From Stephen the early Christian martyrs followed in the steps of their master and forgave their enemies right up to the Martin Luther Kings of the twentieth century and the twenty-first. There are an uncountable number of forgiving compassionate Christians who will never hit the headlines. It is also true that there are loving and compassionate Muslims who express grace and mercy. What Massadie does highlight, however, is how the concept of evil, the Devil, is used to bring about untold suffering, by calling anyone who does not follow one's own particular creed or party – 'of the Devil'! When this happens, then human beings are defacing the image in which they were created.

> If we think of God at all worthily, we cannot help thinking of him as working for high and worthy ends. Therefore we cannot help thinking of him, as in creation, working for some end worthy of himself. But what end does the popular creed assign to him? A creation mutilated, ruined, and that for ever. A creation ending in misery and endless sin to infinite numbers of the created; and all this misery and horror brought into sharper relief by a vain and fruitless attempt to save all: by a purpose of love declared to all, and yet not in fact reaching all: a creation which is but the portal to hell for so many of the created. And you gravely ask thoughtful enquirers to believe this; to believe that, contemplating these horrors destined never to cease, the morning stars are described as singing together, and all the sons of God shouting for joy on the morning of creation.
>
> The sons of God shouted for joy, as they contemplated creation; but they should have wept had the popular creed been true. For that creed represents the present life as darkened by the prospect of evil triumphant; our present sorrows made keener by the prospect of a future life, which will be, not to the wicked merely, but to the whole race of man, an evil and a curse – a life which every good man would, if he could, bring to an instant end. To prove this, I will take a definite example. Further, I will concede to the advocates of the popular creed one point of very considerable importance (to which they have no right), e.g., that the number of the saved greatly exceeds the lost. Suppose it were offered to the father of three children to take his choice whether two should be received into Heaven and one condemned to hell,

or the whole should be annihilated in death. What would a parent say? Where is the father who would dare to secure the bliss of two children at the cost of the endless misery of one? Which of the family would he select as the victim, whose undying pain should secure his brother's immortal joy? Is there anyone living who would not suffer himself and his children to sink back again into nothingness, rather than purchase heaven at such a price? Now, if so, if we should so act in the case of our own children, we are bound morally to make the same choice with respect to everyone. No moral being would consent to purchase eternal happiness at the price of another's eternal woe.[24]

In our next chapter we shall consider the attitude of Jesus, the founder of the Christian faith, to the question of hell.

---

[24] *Universalism Asserted*, T Allin, 1895 William & Norgate, pp. 54–55. In the 19th Century the term 'the popular creed' referred to those who held to a 'nature of Hell' as eternal punishment.

Chapter 2: Christ and Hell

We have the oft quoted comment 'that Jesus himself taught more about hell than anyone else in scripture.'[25] I challenge this assertion; teaching is not limited to words.

If we therefore look at the whole of the Lord Jesus' ministry, words, attitudes and actions, the emphasis is on mercy, and even his words emphasise mercy over and above judgement. You should not isolate Christ's words from his attitudes and actions; words are actions, actions are words, and we must not take the sheer amount of words as an indication that emphasises that particular aspect of teaching above others. For example, the Scribes and Pharisees had written reams on the Law, words upon words. You could say they had written more about the Law than anyone else. Jesus however sums up all their words in just two commands: 'Love the Spirit' (God) and 'Love your neighbour.'[26] Those few words were not limited to the letter of the Law but to the spirit of the Law.[27] A few words can sometimes speak volumes; the fact that Jesus said i.e. used more 'words' about hell than others, is no indication that he 'taught' more about hell than any others. He actually taught more about mercy, forgiveness, compassion, understanding; he taught more about love in action, and indeed it was his 'action' ultimately on the cross that declared the emphasis of his whole ministry – which was love and mercy, not judgement. He turned the judgement in upon himself,[28] that

---

[25] 'The Nature of Hell', from the Foreword to the Evangelical Alliance Report p.xiii.

[26] Mark 12:31.

[27] Spirit over and above human and divine Law is seen when Jesus broke the Sabbath Laws; for as we read in James, mercy triumphs over judgement (2:13).

[28] The judgement that is proclaimed and exercised in life to varying degrees as recorded in the Old Testament is all summed up and finally poured out upon God, the Spirit of creation himself in the human body of Christ. Throughout the Old Testament, even in the midst of judgements there is a constant theme of mercy. This is an orthodox Christian position.

it would not be turned in upon us who could not bear it. His final words, though few, on the cross, even in his agony, declare his mercy and forgiveness pouring forth from his love: 'Father, forgive them, they know not what they do.'[29] Is this not asking for forgiveness even for those who at that time are not asking for it themselves?

This being so, it surely is mercy, it is Jesus putting into action his own words, which are action: 'love your enemies'. At the Last Supper, Jesus did teach with words at some length; but words, few or many, are not the criteria for where the emphasis lies. The significance lies in the content, the meaning of the words used. Christ's whole life, in fact, and ultimately his action on the cross 'spoke' and 'taught'. It included words, precious words, but words that could not be divorced from action, and ultimately it was his attitude in life and in death that finally and for ever proclaimed where his emphasis lay. At the Last Supper, having taught with words, he then taught in action, he knelt down and washed their feet – an action, an attitude that 'spoke' volumes.

The attitude of Jesus is expressed again and again in his compassion for the multitudes, in words, attitudes and action (Matthew 9:35-36 and Mark 6:34), and Paul takes hold of Christ's attitude as he writes to the Colossians (3:12–14):

> Therefore, as God's chosen people, holy and dearly loved, clothe yourselves with compassion, kindness, humility, gentleness and patience. Bear with each other and forgive whatever grievances you may have against one another. And over all these virtues put on love, which binds them all together in perfect unity.

Looking at what is generally regarded as the very first Gospel written, we discover the very first words Jesus preaches at the commencement of his ministry are words of hope, of good news: 'The time has come, the kingdom of God is near. Repent and believe the good news.' (Mark 1:15). To repent is to move in a new direction; now we can enter upon a wonderful new beginning, a new direction, in good times and bad times, sickness and health, tears and laughter. We can move in them and through them on a

---

[29] Luke 23:34.

new path – it's the path of love, which issues in justice, mercy, understanding and forgiveness, what the good news gives, and what the good news wants us to naturally flow over into the lives of others.

This is good news, and it is about life. Then we discover, after his choosing the disciples, Jesus' first recorded act in Mark's record is to cast out evil, do away with that which spoils and destroys life, and a man is delivered from his oppression, Mark 1:23-25. He taught with words and action. He came to deliver mankind from the oppressions that grip the human soul, spirit, mind, as indeed was prophesied concerning Christ by the Prophet, Isaiah:

> The spirit of the Sovereign Lord is upon me, because he has anointed me to preach good news to the poor. He has sent me to bind up the broken-hearted, to proclaim freedom for the captives… instead of mourning, a garment of praise instead of a spirit of despair…[30]

Then, as we go through this Gospel in the order in which events are recorded, we find him again healing; this time Simon's mother-in-law, plus healing and curing people of evil oppression in the evening (Mark 1:29–34). He was pouring out love, good news, mercy and judgement, day and night; the judgement was on the evil that was oppressing people which he was casting out – good news indeed. There was no condemnation yet on people, only on that which was hurting them, destroying their lives; for he came to give life. We find him turning aside to rest in prayer (Mark 1:35). We read of him again teaching and driving out evil, (Mark 1:38-39).

And so it goes on. He heals a leper, and we read that Jesus was filled with compassion for him (Mark 1:41). Then we have the account of a man too weak to come himself to Jesus, so his friends bring him, and for the first time in this Gospel, we are left in no doubt where his emphasis lay. It lay over and above any law; it

---

[30] Isaiah 61:1–3. We note that when Jesus quotes from this passage he does not include v.2: 'to proclaim the year of the Lord's favour and the day of vengeance of our God'. I suggest, because this was *not* the emphasis of his ministry, he had come primarily to bring hope, love and life, mercy and forgiveness.

was motivated by love. The emphasis was the forgiveness of sin, even in the face of criticism and opposition from the religious teachers of the day. His compassion went beyond the physical to the healing of the spirit through forgiveness (Mark 2:1–12).

Then again we see his compassion for outsiders, as he has a meal at Levi's house, among all the 'sinners' that gathered there. And Jesus replies with more of the good news: 'It is not the healthy who need a doctor, but the sick. I have not come to call the righteous but sinners.' (Mark 2:17).

In Mark 2:23–27 we find Jesus sensitively interpreting the Law, as he allows his disciples to eat the heads of grain in a corn-field, and when criticised he draws upon the Old Testament scriptures for instance when David broke the Law; for the words of the Law made bold statements but the spirit of the Law took in particular circumstances and operated on the principle of mercy motivated by love. This principle is again emphasised in Chapter 3, with the account of the man with the withered hand. Jesus asks: 'Which is lawful on the Sabbath, to do good or to do evil, to save life or to kill?' (Mark 3:4). They in their hearts were seeking to take life – his; while he was giving life, good news – that was his emphasis, that was his mission.

He was accused of being evil, doing wrong because he was breaking traditions and laws that were held sacred, again and again. Ultimately he would be prepared to be cursed by their own laws, because in his love and mercy he would be hung on a tree, crucified. There indeed mercy triumphed over judgement. It is not until we are halfway through this Gospel that we have any record whatsoever of eternal punishment (Mark 9). Similar texts that appear to support eternal punishment shall be looked at later – see Chapter 3 on 'The Meaning of Hell'.

The next passage on judgement comes in Chapter 13 of Mark's Gospel, but there is no mention of eternal punishment here. In fact, in the whole of Mark's Gospel, it is only in one short passage in Chapter 9 that there is any mention by Jesus of eternal punishment. It is significant that if, as is widely held, this Gospel was teamwork, Peter sharing with Mark his three years with Jesus of Nazareth, we know he was well aware of the love, mercy and forgiveness of Christ, for he had denied and disowned Christ with curses at the time when Jesus needed him most; Peter knew that mercy triumphs over judgement (James 2:13).

In his book, *What does the Bible really say about Hell?* Randolph Klassen writes:

> A member of one congregation I served chided me for not preaching about hell. My reticence reflected, no doubt, a general nervousness among clergy today to preach about hell, so my response to him was admittedly trite. Since I knew some members had to endure a sort of hell each week, I said I would rather give them a good dose of Heaven on Sunday! My preference is to follow the example of the Bethlehem angel whose message was, 'good news of great joy for all people' (Luke 2:10); to me this is being 'ev-angel-ical'. I want to be that kind of 'angel messenger'.[31]

My primary motivation is to share a view of God that is in harmony with Jesus Christ. The living word of God, Jesus, is our best guide to understanding the inspired written word of God. The Reverend W A Criswell wishes to defend biblical authority when he says the Bible, 'is the writing of the living God. Each sentence was dictated by God's Holy Spirit.'. Klassen, however, thinks this dishonours God:

> Was Jesus wrong when he said of the temple, 'You see all these …truly not one stone will be left here upon another; all will be thrown down.' Matthew 24:2. Archaeologists uncovered the awful devastation – but parts of the walls – some stones still rested on the lower ones as originally built. The literalist must concede that Jesus erred. But when one recognises Jesus' frequent use of hyperbole, his statement is true. If God dictated scripture, why is his grammar less than perfect in Mark? His numbers inconsistent, where the same events are recorded in Kings and Chronicles? Women judged more harshly than men in Exodus? The point I want to emphasise… in many instances we are already practising principles of interpretation that respect the limitations of language that recognise variant literary forms, and that appreciate the role cultural context plays in getting at the true meaning of a passage.
>
> We know the events in Genesis predate written history, so we

---

[31] *What does the Bible really say about hell?* pp. 17–18, Pandora Press, 1984.

do not expect eyewitness accuracy from an oral tradition. We recognise the Psalms as songs and prayers in poetic form. The literary form of the Gospels is mainly narrative; the apostles' letters to churches often addressing known situations.[32]

It must also be recognised of course that the Bible is 'oriental'. It breathes the spirit of the East, with its hyperboles and metaphors, what seem to us so often as gross exaggerations. Surely we do not take literally 'to hate my father and mother'.[33]

If it is understanding we seek we do need to wrestle with the text, delve into its cultural and historical context, its linguistic form. It is not all easy to understand; indeed, Peter had trouble understanding Paul's writings (2 Peter 3:16).

Randy Klassan states:

> ...The biggest problem with taking the whole Bible as the verbally dictated word of God is that it puts the text of scripture above the living word of God, Jesus Christ. Many verses in the Bible clearly are contradicted by the manner and message of Jesus. In Leviticus, a child who curses his parents is to be put to death (Lev 20:9). Jesus does not support that form of discipline. Let Jesus be Lord of scripture, not the reverse![34]

Many people reading the Bible will not have the training or ability to read scripture with an understanding of the original languages in which it was written. While we are greatly indebted to the work of scholars, as has been made clear in these pages. There has to be a way of understanding scripture for those who are not able or do not have the time to delve into all the cultural linguistic and historical context, crucial though these are. For me, it is this: if any passage does not accord with the general ethos of Jesus' ministry, in his words, attitudes and actions of love and compassion, seen supremely in his words from a cross, where he pours out his love

---

[32] Ibid., pp. 17, 18.

[33] Though I would not want to take these at all as the words of Jesus. Taken as hyperbole, it seems to me Jesus is emphasising how agape love is so much deeper than even love for father and mother; in fact it is agape love which enhances all other loves, enriches them, in its consideration of the needs of others as well as one's own.

[34] *What does the Bible really say about hell?* 2001, p.78.

on all including his enemies, in forgiveness, then they cannot be the words of Jesus. Taking his words at face value, would Jesus tell us to hate father or mother when he also tells us to love even our enemies? How could such a one speak of torturing his enemies forever, or of having them annihilated?

Besides the exegetical challenges to the view of a hell which promotes eternal punishment or annihilation, there is the ethical problem, which is even greater. Klassan writes:

> Jesus revealed a love and grace in God unparalleled in any religion or philosophy. It was so amazing, John had to write, 'God is love.' (1 John 4:16) No interpretation of God that differs, challenges, or contradicts this view can be considered valid. Again I refer to Clark Pinnock's statement:
>
> 'Everlasting torture is intolerable from a moral point of view because it pictures God acting like a bloodthirsty monster who maintains an everlasting Auschwitz for his enemies whom he does not allow to die. How can one love a God like that?'
>
> An eternal hell poses the problem of a glaring inconsistency in the character of God. There is an affront to an enlightened sense of justice. There is also the matter of what purpose is served by it all. Finally, the question can be raised about whose victory is finally won if most people are in hell.
>
> While the Bible recognises God as holy and therefore as requiring justice, it does not see God as being vindictive or wanting to punish. A description of God recurring in the Bible is expressed in these words:
>
> 'His anger is but for a moment; his favour is everlasting. Weeping may linger for the night, but joy comes with the morning,' (Psalm 30:5)
>
> 'He will not always accuse nor will he keep his anger forever. He does not deal with us according to our sins, nor repay us according to our iniquities.' (Psalm 103:9–10)[35]

We shall now turn to the actual meaning of the word 'hell'.

---

[35] Ibid. p. 84.

Chapter 3: The Meaning of Hell

What does this word, hell, mean? What is its history? It is not a Biblical word, it was never in the original autographs (documents, texts) of scripture.

The word 'hell' did not exist in the Bible until the seventeenth century. The word 'hell' has an interesting history, it is a very poor and misleading translation of the words, Tartarus, Sheol, Hades and Gehenna.

Let us take a look at the English word 'hell' to see what it meant when the Authorised Version of the Bible was produced. The word meant a 'hole', the unseen; it simply meant 'the unseen place'; it also meant 'the covered place'. Archbishop Usher, in his answer to a Jesuit, informs us that the Anglo-Saxon helan meant 'to cover', so 'to hell the head' meant 'to put on a hat', and a 'hellier' was a slater. And even right up to the early twentieth century in the south of England a thatcher was called a 'hellier', one who covers in a house. It was also a word used in games. On village greens in seventeenth century England a 'hell' was to be found, a hideout where in village games the girls would run to avoid being kissed. It was also a name given to the place under the Exchequer Chamber where the King's debtors were kept; and it was also used to describe the place where the tailor threw his shreds.

So it can be seen that the word 'hell' had none of the terrible meanings that came to be associated with it, and which it has today. So the translators of the authorised version of the Bible translated 'Hades' or 'Sheol', Gehenna and Tartarus with the English word 'hell'. But it has become very misleading in these later days. The Revised Version however corrects this error. 'His soul was not left in Hades (not hell), nor did his flesh see corruption' (Acts 2:31); and again in Revelation 1:18, 'I have the keys of death and of Hades'; and in Revelation 20:13, 'death and Hades gave up the dead'. And it is 'in Hades' (not hell) that 'the rich man' in Luke 16:23 'lifts up his eyes, being in torment'.

Now why this is all so important is because, as we shall see later, to the Jewish mind these words – Gehenna, Hades, Sheol or Tartarus – never had the meaning of 'everlasting', and as we shall see when we come to examine the word 'aeonian', neither does this necessarily carry the meaning endless; and furthermore, when we look at the word 'damnation' and its derivatives, we note it is not used once in the Old Testament, and in the New Testament the uses are exceptional and arbitrary translations of two Greek verbs or their derivatives, which occur 308 times, apollumi and krino. The Authorised Version translates these Greek verbs as 'damnation'. To see how unreasonable this is, we only have to look at some examples in scripture where it is used:

'A young widow who marries again must be damned to endless torments' (1 Tim 5:12), 'having damnation', (krima); although Paul expressly recommends young widows to do so two verses later on. It is to say that everyone who ever eats the Lord's Supper unworthily, eats and drinks 'eternal punishment' to himself, though Paul adds, almost in the next verse that judgement (krima) is disciplinary or educational (paideuometha).[36]

Once we grasp the fact that damnation does not naturally or necessarily mean damned to eternal punishment, much of what is built on in the Evangelical Alliance's report flounders on sinking sand. In the report the word hell is predicted as being endless, which is not predicted for Sheol or Hades, Gehenna or (in one place, 2 Peter 2:4) Tartarus.

The Evangelical Alliance's report concedes that the term 'Gehenna' does not specifically refer to duration. After quoting texts in the New Testament in the synoptics where it is found, always on the lips of Jesus Christ, it goes on: 'None of the above verses specifically mentions the duration of Gehenna; neither do they specify its function in terms of punishment.'[37]

In the AV (Authorised Version, King James Bible) the word 'hell' is used for 'Sheol' in such passages as, 'you will not leave my

---

[36] The original meaning of 'damnation' was much milder. For example, an Act passed when John Russell was Chancellor (in the reign of Richard III or Henry VII) stated that sanction of an act against extorted benevolences is called a 'damnation', that is, an infliction of loss, and of course this original meaning is still found in such words as 'demnify', 'indemnify', and 'indemnity'.

[37] 'The Nature of Hell', Acute, pp. 43–44.

soul in Hell', Psalm 16:10 (the dim underworld, or abode of the dead – Acts 2:27–31). In such a passage as this, there is surely no more reason to translate 'Sheol' by hell than there would be in changing Genesis 37:35 to read 'I will go down into hell, unto my son, mourning'. It is one of the saddest things in the English language that every Sunday people in church who use the 1662 Prayer Book edition, still recite from the creed this incredible error, 'He descended into Hell' – when the word is Hades, Sheol.

'Sheol' occurs in the Old Testament sixty-five times; and in the AV it is translated as 'hell' thirty-one times, and the 'grave' thirty one times; yet the words 'grave' and 'hell' are poles apart. One brings to mind endless torment, the other of final rest and cessation of pain.

It is incredible that a word so full of meaning such as Sheol should be substituted even by such a word as 'grave', which is fairly bland and colourless; and it is indeed criminal to substitute 'Sheol' for 'hell'; it has been said that Sheol 'is a term as opposite to hell, as light is to darkness'.[38]

It is equally unsatisfactory to translate 'Hell' for 'Hades'. Eleven times this word occurs in the New Testament. In none of the eleven does it mean 'hell'. Again for that famous passage in Luke 16:23, the rendering, 'In hell he lifted up his eyes, being in torments', once we use 'in Hades' (not Hell), then at once all the false conclusions that have been deduced from this passage are dissipated.

'Hell' is also used to translate 'Tartarus' in 2 Peter 2:4: 'For God did not spare angels when they sinned, but sent them to hell' (NIV). But Peter is expressly referring to a temporary state not endless punishment, for he goes on to say – 'to be held in judgement'.

Their time of judgement has not come, and by that time they may well have turned in a fresh direction in attitude – hence having an opportunity for repentance.

Next we come to the word 'Gehenna'. The word means Valley of Hinnom.[39] It is mentioned thirteen times in the Old

---

[38] Quoted by F W Farrar from the author Olav Haneschamoth, in *Mercy and Judgement*, p. 372.
[39] Sometimes referred to as 'The son (or sons) of Hinnom'.

Testament, and in not one of these passages does it mean 'hell'.[40] In the New Testament 'Gehenna' is referred to by the Lord Jesus Christ seven times in Matthew (5:22, 29, 30; 10:28; 18:9; 23:15,33); three times in Mark, and once in Luke (12:5); and once in James 3:6. In none of these passages is it called endless. The only possible exception is found in Mark 9:43-48 viz., 'the worm that does not die and where fire is not quenched'.

These however are purely metaphorical expressions and in fact are borrowed directly from a metaphor of Isaiah respecting earthly consequences (Isaiah 66:24).

Seven of the ten references to 'Gehenna' come out of one single passage from one single discourse, recorded in Matthew 5, and repeated in part in Matthew 18 and Mark 9, and it is more than likely that in all seven references the primary allusion is to an earthly Jewish punishment, and hence finite and limited in duration.

The word 'Gehenna' does not occur once in all the thirteen letters of Paul, and 'Hades' occurs only once, though in fact he had declared to his converts 'the whole counsel of God'; and it does not occur once in John's letters or the letters of Hebrews or in those of Peter.

And we note that Paul and Peter had received much mercy and understanding from Jesus Christ – Paul, a one-time persecutor of Christians, the other a disciple who had denied Jesus when he needed him most. Jesus exemplifies mercy over judgement. Paul and Peter both knew this from their own experience.

Origen, one of the few Fathers of the Church who studied Hebrew for the sole purpose of interpreting scripture, informs us that he had discovered by research what the Jews really meant by Gehenna; and that Celsus and others (like most today) talked of it with no knowledge of its significance.

---

[40] Five times used of the valley outside Jerusalem that in ancient times had been, and later became, known as the pleasant Valley of Hinnom. Joshua 15:8, 18:16; Nehemiah 11:30. Three times it is mentioned as having defiled by the burning of human beings alive Moloch worship under Ahaz and Manasseh (2 Chronicles 28:3, 33:6; 2 Kings 23:10). Five times in reference to God's wrath against the abomination of cruelly burning human beings, and especially infants, with fire; expressing his abhorrence as a thing 'which never came into his mind' (Jeremiah 7:31, 32; 18:1–15; 22:35). How then could anyone imagine that God would do this to any one 'everlastingly'?

Apart from its primary meaning of the Valley of Hinnom outside Jerusalem, it had come, he said, to acquire a secondary meaning of purificatory punishment, and there he stops with the mysterious remark that he 'does not think it wise to dwell any further on his discoveries'. It's possible of course that it could have led to more persecution for him.[41]

F W Farrar continues, 'it is impossible to doubt that he had discovered that normally the Jews did not apply the word to an endless but a terminable state.'[42]

Dame Cecily Saunders, the pioneer of the hospice movement, who has helped many to set out on their final journey, said this about hell:

> As for hell, I can imagine turning away into my own darkness, but I hate to think of anyone else doing it. However, I certainly don't think that I'm fit as I am now to step into eternity. I hope that something will happen to make me fit to do so, and I suppose that is what is meant by purgatory. It seems to me most helpful. Judgement, you know, means setting things right; it doesn't just mean punishment.[43]

I would wish to include within the hope of the Gospel an intermediate state (not necessarily purgatory, which we shall look at later in Chapter 8), a place of continued pilgrimage, with an understanding of judgement, the purpose of which is to set things right both personally and cosmically, leading to a final restitution.

Speaking of Christ, the scriptures inform us:

> For God was pleased to have all his fullness dwell in him, and through him to reconcile to himself all things, whether things on earth or things in heaven, by making peace through his blood, shed on the cross. (Col. 1:19–20).

---

[41] Ibid. pp. 375–376.

[42] Ibid.

[43] Quoted in Gerald Priestland's book, *Priestland's Progress*, pp. 198–199, BBC, 1981.

Chapter 4: Eternal Destiny – Tradition and Hell

In the foreword to the E A's report on hell, we read that it

> ...Aims to inform those who have not thought through the issue yet, but also offers those with strong convictions an opportunity to test their stance once more against the Biblical witness, rather than against tradition, or culture alone.[44]

I recognise the great sincerity and genuine Christian love that the Reverend Joel Edwards wishes to express with a profound commitment to the faith; but sadly, I would suggest that the Evangelical Alliance's report itself is in fact based more on tradition than on scripture. Let me illustrate by quoting again from the report:

> ...As evangelicals ourselves we affirm that all teaching on what happens after death must be based primarily on scripture, that it must pay serious regard to the historic creeds and confessions of the church down the centuries, and that it must give particular attention to the theologies of the reformation and post-reformation Protestantism, *since it is these theologies which have most distinctly shaped evangelical belief as we know it today.*[45]

While it is stated that what happens after death must be based primarily on scripture, it appears from what follows that the scriptures are themselves interpreted through the spectacles of reformation and post-reformation theologies.

Reaction to the corrupt practices of the Roman Catholic Church of the day, which of course the Reformation was, swung the pendulum so far in the opposite direction to 'works' as the way to salvation, that a tradition grew up from which we still

---

[44] From the Foreword 'The Nature of Hell' p. xiv.
[45] Ibid. from p. 111 (The italicising is mine).

suffer, so that 'good works' have little or no place as far as salvation is concerned. They are only regarded as an expression of the life of the believer, indeed a crucial expression, but none the less still an expression not the essence of salvation. So that as already noted – a point which I wish to emphasise – a person who has led a good life, giving themselves in the cause of humanity, but who has not 'accepted Christ', is doomed to a lost eternity. However, a person who has 'accepted Christ', but who in comparison to the former has given little time in love and care for others has, none the less, eternal life and goes to Heaven. This concept of salvation seems to ignore most of the biblical texts, in both the Old and New Testaments.

For example, see Matthew 25:34–36, and Micah 6:6–8, where the emphasis is on action, and mercy, not on regarding oneself as a member of the covenant people of God divorced from action.

The Evangelical Alliance's report, as noted, lays stress on the importance of the theologies of Reformation and post-Reformation theologies, but these are open to strong criticisms. For example, Sierd Woudstra finds real weaknesses in the three traditional reformed confessions: the Belgic Confession, the Heidelberg Catechism, and the Canons of Dort. He writes:

> Loath as I am to go against so venerable a document as the Heidelberg Catechism, it seems to me that Bonda's point is well taken. The reformed creeds, resting on their spiritual fathers St Augustine and John Calvin, are, it seems to me, seriously flawed. The Biblical perspective, as Bonda points out, is that of a God who goes out in search of the one sheep that became lost, not that of a God who elects some to everlasting life, bypassing all others and sending them to a never-ending 'death'.[46]

Yet it appears these doctrines are still held tenaciously by loving, compassionate Christians in the mindset of the sixteenth century reaction to the Roman Catholic Church of the day. Should we not rather bend over backwards to believe in the salvation of the many? Rather than bend over backwards to advocate the loss of the many in eternal punishment or annihilation?

---

[46] From the Foreword to *The One Purpose of God* p. xx.

F W Farrar, caught up in the debates on hell and eternal destiny in the nineteenth century, writes:

> Is there any human being to whom it would not be an infamy to confess that he did not wish that it were true that all men might be ultimately saved, as it is God's will (1 Timothy 2:4) that they should be saved? ...do we wish that any soul of man should suffer endless torments? If not, we are surely permitted to pay respectful attention to the arguments of those who think themselves entitled by scripture to believe that which we too desire, but scarcely even dare to hope.[47]

There are some today of course who believe that denial of eternal punishment is not a biblical but an emotional response. For example, Dr James Packer, one of the most ardent defenders of the doctrine of eternal punishment, a man who has been a blessing to many through his lectures and written works, believes that to disbelieve in eternal punishment is more an emotional response than a scriptural one. Commenting on the annihilationist and conditional immortality views, he writes:

> Its advocates appear to back into it in horrified recoil from the thought of millions in endless distress rather than move into it because the obvious meaning of scripture beckons them.[48]

Not to recoil at such a doctrine would indeed be strange and somewhat inhuman, for to suffer untold distress with never ever any release is surely something far worse than even the concentration camps of Nazi Germany.

J I Packer also writes the Foreword to Dr Larry Dixon's book, *The Other Side of the Good News* (an unfortunate title, it being a contradiction in terms, for it makes the 'good news' partly bad

---

[47] F W Farrar, *Mercy and Judgement*. pp. 8–9; MacMillan, 1881.

[48] J I Packer, *Crux*, Regent College, Sept 90, Vol xxvi. No 3. Quoted by Dr Bruce Milne on p. 71 in *Preaching the Word* – addresses from the Evangelical Assembly. Also quoted in 'The Problem of Eternal Punishment', an address given by J I Packer on the Leon Morris Lecture for the Evangelical Alliance (Victoria) on Friday 31st August 1990, in Blackburn North Baptist Church, Melbourne, Australia; not once in this lecture is the crucial subject of suffering in this world linked in with the nature of hell.

news which eclipses its good news). He uses the following words:

> To believe what the Bible appears to say about human destiny
> apart from the grace of God is a bitter pill indeed, and no one
> should wonder that attempts are made to explore alternative
> understanding of God's revelation on this topic. It is suggested
> that the Bible is unclear, or incoherent, or inconsistent, or
> untrustworthy, when it speaks of the outcome of judgement after
> death, or alternatively that virtually the whole church has for two
> thousand years misunderstood the texts. Are any of these
> suggestions plausible? I do not think so, nor does Dr Dixon. He
> has mounted an argument that, however disconcerting, must be
> reckoned with in any future discussion of biblical teaching on
> human destiny. I for one, am grateful for his work, and commend
> it to all who are willing to be biblically rational on this sombre
> subject.

I would echo those last words, for the work that F W Farrar and Jan
Bonda have done on this 'sombre subject'. By way of comment on J
I Packer's Foreword to Dr Dixon's book, I would suggest a reading
of F W Farrar's *Mercy and Judgment*, with regard to Dr Packer's
observation 'that virtually the whole church has for two thousand
years misunderstood the texts'. Farrar draws attention to a host of
writers over the centuries, as we shall see, including fathers of the
church, who accept the view of a wider hope.[49] Of course, Farrar is
out of print now, and that is why I believe he should be seen in
print again.

Something both F W Farrar and Jan Bonda have very much in
common is the fact that they are both committed to the authority
of scripture, and their response is, not only an emotional one,
understandable though that surely is; it is also a biblical one. They
are both biblically minded. They do not suggest that the Bible is
unclear, incoherent or inconsistent or untrustworthy when it
speaks of the outcome of judgment after death.

Both are committed to a sound exegetical study of the scriptures, both accept the authority of the scriptures, both have firm

---

[49] See Appendix. Farrar draws attention to many who held to a wider hope, many
intimating salvation for all, others that there is opportunity beyond the grave to
respond to the Gospel.

ground for believing in a wider hope than Dr Packer and Dr Dixon allow.

I would suggest that Dr Packer and Dr Dixon are in danger of allowing theological traditions to have the final word, rather than allowing tradition to find its proper place in relation to scripture.

Chapter 5: The Ethos of Scripture

It is important to see scripture as a whole. What is its general ethos?

Where do we find its main thrust, its overall objective? The Bible can be called a record of salvation history. It talks of judgment and punishment for wrongdoing, but again and again we read of restoration.

Not all the answers to human existence are given in the Bible; we are not told why evil should ever have been allowed to enter into creation. But what we are told is how evil is dealt with. We are given a pattern for life in the present and an awareness of the immensity of life, so vast that it goes on beyond the grave.

The Bible focuses on being saved now from all that would destroy life. It begins with creation and ends with recreation. The first book in the Bible, Genesis, records this in poetic form, and the book of Revelation, the last book in the Bible, concludes with an account of the new creation through a vision. In between is the history of how to live now with an increasing awareness of a dimension beyond, learning to live the life of eternity now, as we say in the Lord's Prayer, 'thy kingdom come… on earth as it is in heaven'. We begin a spiritual pilgrimage which goes on beyond the grave.

The Bible focuses on the fortunes of one nation through whom all the world will be blessed, not because it is better than any other, but because that is the way the spirit's plan is unfolded through grace – undeserved favour, which extends to the whole world to all nations. Out of the one nation emerges a Messiah, the Christ, Jesus of Nazareth, through whom all the nations of the world would be blessed. His purpose is nothing less than the salvation of the whole created order. It is not judgement but mercy, reconstruction not destruction; that is the main thrust of scripture. If there were to be allowed a hell of everlasting punishment, it would seem that evil had won. The symbol of all evil, the

Devil, had secured some souls for ever in everlasting destruction and torment. But this is not the case. Eternal love will be victorious, with wholeness and healing for the whole created order.

Sadly, however, some have believed that destruction will continue and ultimate healing for some, perhaps many, will not take place; such a doctrine does tend to draw the conclusion that the spirit, God, will not reconcile to himself all things. But the truth is that God will reconcile to himself all things. (Col 1:19)

Some have suggested that to weaken the doctrine of destruction, fear of eternal punishment, is to weaken the call to mission, as if the call to righteousness born of love were not a sufficient reason for mission now. As if fear were more powerful than love. But can we not say it was love for the world that overcame Christ's fear of the cross, and he therefore drank the cup of suffering? Or that in spite of that fear he still went to the cross, because he loved?

Surely there is an urgent need right now for hatred, fear of destruction and so on to be replaced by love and righteousness; so that people are just in their dealings with each other, forgiving and merciful, understanding and loving; so that love replaces hate. There is an urgent call for exercising that love which Christ spoke of right now, mercy that triumphs over judgement, love that disciplines with a view to restoration and salvation.

Preachers have said, again and again, that if there be no endless hell, such as they conceive and represent, it would not be worth any man's while to preach at all. Rob them of their pictures of future horror, and they seem to have no lever left wherewith to move mankind! Strange that for four thousand years the Most High by His servants – while He ever pointed out the natural consequences of sin – revealed no such terror, appealed to no such motives! In all those books of the Old Testament there are but four texts which, even by stretching them on the rack of an impossible exegesis, can be made even to seem to bear witness to the Augustinian, mediaeval, and modern views of hell. Neither Moses, nor Samuel, nor Elijah, nor Elisha, nor the writers of the historical books, nor Ezra, nor Nehemiah, nor the Sweet Psalmist of Israel, nor fourteen out of the sixteen Prophets have one word to say which, even when they speak of retribution, can by the most violent and unreasonable methods be made to say a word about endless torments. And the popular theology, which is declared to be so potent, is, on the contrary, so wholly inefficacious, that it has been taught for centuries with this result, that it is unhappily the standing jest alike of the ablest and of the coarsest of those who would be assumed to need it most as an element of terror.

But further, out of these four texts in the whole Old Testament which can alone be forced by any competent critic into the service of Calvinistic eschatology, three are so absolutely irrelevant that to adduce them at all can only prove how feeble are the weapons which can be snatched up for misuse by a despairing cause.[50]

Fear of punishment is a tool that tyrants and terrorists have used to further their ends – Stalin, Hitler and Saddam Hussein, for example. As the Bible unfolds, it develops the theme of indestructible love which outlasts all (Romans 8, 1 Cor. 13), and which is the ultimate answer for humanity. This love is so powerful that even in apparent weak and hopeless situations it is victorious (as Maximillian Kolbe showed in the concentration camp).[51] This is the love that one day will be all encompassing. For Christ, in a final and what looked like a hopeless situation, in utter weakness and in the final failure of a human body – death – brought victory on the cross; love overcame hate.

One of the main themes of Paul's letter to the Romans is 'righteousness' – Romans 1:17: 'In the Gospel a righteousness from God is revealed, a righteousness that is by faith from first to last, just as it is written, "The righteous will live by faith".' (Though it is, as we shall see, love that is the motivating power for righteousness and salvation.) Faith is of course trust, even when you can't work everything out. From the earliest times Israel has worshipped Jahweh as the one who directs his universal gift of righteousness to them. The idea that this would at the same time be a threat to Israel is untenable. There is no such concept as 'punishing righteousness'. The term 'punishing' would contradict the very idea of 'righteousness' (Gerhard von Rad). For Paul, righteousness is in

---

[50] *Mercy and Judgement*, p. 436.
[51] From *Saints of the Twentieth Century*, Brother Kenneth, CGA, Mowbrays, 1976 pp. 97–98.

harmony with the Old Judaist tradition, which sees it 'not only as an ethical attribute of God and/or of mankind, instead with reference to humans, it is an essential characteristic of that which allows man to be what he should be in relationship to God and mankind.'

It is God's intention in righteousness to save, not destroy humanity. So what about the Old Testament record of whole groups of people being destroyed? Now this always refers to physical destruction – never spiritual destruction. We have a classic example in Sodom (Genesis 18) where we read of the physical destruction of Sodom, but in Ezekiel 16 we read of the salvation of Sodom – its restoration.

In Deuteronomy 20:16 we read of Israel being told to destroy her enemies: 'do not leave alive anything that breathes. This could be taken as the writer being carried away with extreme nationalistic feelings and not God's words. In Deuteronomy, we read of God telling the Israelites 'to love those who are aliens, for you yourselves were aliens in Egypt.' This is repeated in Leviticus 19, 'the alien living with you must be treated as one of your native born. Love him as yourself.' Even the disciples after Christ's resurrection were still looking for an earthly kingdom (Acts 1:6). Christ spoke of his kingdom not of this world.

Righteousness is a love word, not exclusively a punishment word. In scripture the righteousness of God is always a saving righteousness. The worldly powers have always been good at destruction; God, the Spirit, is in the business of salvation, restoration.

From the cross, words from the Bible were quoted, words of hopelessness and words of hopefulness. Thus in that one moment they sum up the dilemma of humanity, and in the summing up offering the wonderful gift of forgiveness: 'My God, my God, why have you forsaken me?' and 'Father, forgive them, they know not what they do.' These are caring words to strangers, those who were actually responsible for Jesus being there, and words of comfort to those close to him, his mother and a disciple (John), as he gives them a personal word of comfort, reminding them they are not left alone, giving them to each other in mutual care, John 19:25–27.

Christ knew the fellowship of humanity's forsakenness and

articulates it in quoting scripture, and then proclaims the main thrust of scripture with amazing words of forgiveness – even for those who were not asking for it themselves. These are words of hope, not only for the thief who cries out to be remembered by Christ, and is told he will be in paradise that day (notice not heaven, but paradise – a word used for the intermediate state), but also words of hope for the thief, too bitter to see at that moment the love which was pouring out from the dying body of the man in the centre.

Then we have the final cry of victory: 'It is finished'…and these significant words: 'He gave up the spirit' – which could not be destroyed, and which would receive a new body not limited to time or space, a solid yet spiritual body, not a ghost. And so we have the good news of Christ resurrected, showing us the way that we would follow, a new body, beyond death – as Colossians puts it: 'He [Christ] is the firstborn from among the dead' …the first to show the way out of death, victory over death to new creation, out of death is born life, the plant dies, the seed is planted in the ground, and life is born again. Destruction does not have the last word – life and recreation does.

Colossians 1:19: 'For God was pleased to have all his fullness dwell in him, and through him to reconcile to himself all things, whether things on earth or things in heaven, by making peace through his blood shed on the cross.' It is of course true that Jesus Christ did speak of the consequences of sin as terrible.

John Hick comments:

That Jesus spoke of real suffering and misery, really to be dreaded, which is to come upon men hereafter as a divinely ordained consequence of selfish and cruel deeds performed in this life, is not to be doubted. Nor is it to be doubted that he wanted his hearers to be aware of this inevitable reaction of the moral order upon human wickedness. But that our Lord taught that such misery is to continue through endless time in a perpetual torture inflicted by God cannot safely be affirmed. Between us and Jesus' original meaning there stand the ambiguity of the New Testament word aionios; the uncertainty as to how, if at all, the notion of endless duration might have been expressed in the Aramaic language which Jesus presumably spoke; and evidence of the intrusions of Jewish apocalyptic themes into the developing Gospel tradition. The textual evidence must accordingly be interpreted in the light of wider considerations drawn from Jesus' teaching as the active and sovereign divine love, we shall find incredible and even blasphemous the idea that God plans to inflict perpetual torture upon any of His children.[52]

Christ offers his life of love now, a challenge and an assurance. He pioneers the way of the spirit for life now and beyond death to a new creation for ever and ever, Amen.

But sadly, as we have observed, there are those who have by looking at certain individual passages of scripture appear not see the whole ethos of scripture, which is ultimate salvation and restoration.

As I endeavour to plunge more and more into the academic debate regarding scriptural interpretation, and read the views of theologians, radicals, fundamentalists, liberals, conservative evangelicals, people of equal academic ability taking in some cases widely differing views, and as I meet pastorally with people in various circumstances, I come again and again to the conclusion that the only solid ground for belief for adherents of any religion, or none, is belief in the kind of love Jesus spoke of and demonstrated. When one takes this on to a developing understanding of human destiny it becomes crucial for one to investigate increasingly the concept that the only ultimate reality that created the universe and that holds out a positive hope for the present and for the future, be it in personal or cosmological terms, is love that creates hope for others and oneself, love which seeks the best not only for oneself but others, and which seeks the highest good for all.

Amidst the profusion of opinions, religions, theologies and philosophies I come to no other solid ground than that which spans all, and which coming from a Christian tradition I find in Paul's letter to the Corinthians in Chapter Thirteen: 'Faith, hope and love, these three remain, but the greatest of these is love.' This is the love I see embodied in Jesus of Nazareth who said, amazingly, 'Love your enemies.' This means, looking at Jesus' attitude, that you do not like all that is done by a person, but in love you seek the best for them, wanting them to embrace the foundation for wholesome living – love

---

[52] *Evil and The God of Love,* Collins, Third Impression, 1974 p. 382.

as proclaimed by Jesus. The love that William Barclay expresses thus:

> We must learn to love… Christian love, agape, is that unconquer-
> able benevolence, that undefeatable goodwill, which will never
> seek anything but the highest good of others, no matter what they
> do to us, and no matter how they treat us.

While I certainly do not go along with all the findings in the book
produced by the Jesus seminar entitled *The Five Gospels*, which
attributes so very little authenticity to the recorded words of Christ
in the Gospels, even they regard Christ's words, 'to love one's
enemies' as authentic, and they comment,

> The injunction to love enemies is a memorable aphorism because
> it cuts against the social grain, and constitutes a paradox: 'those
> who love their enemies have no enemies.'[53]

The admonition to 'love thy enemies' is somewhere close to the
very heart of the teaching of Jesus Thus to love one's neighbour as
oneself, to love one's enemy, and the greatest from which the
others spring – to love, 'love', or in other words to love God, spirit,
creative energy – this creative love embraces the physical and
spiritual dovetailed together, when rooted in an understanding of
love as recorded in the words of Jesus. It is when this love is
operated that physical life is enhanced and beautified, and justice
and judgement are exercised through the sieve of love. It is where
mercy triumphs over justice, where actions and attitudes are not
based on legal formulations but on this love proclaimed by Christ.

When one comes to interpreting the Christian scriptures it is
through the sieve of this love that I believe they should be interpreted. It is difficult, if not impossible, to comprehend the horrors
of war as portrayed in parts of the Old Testament, or leaders such
as Joshua killing and plundering, depicting the kind of slaughter
we see in our world today, as God's ordering. For we read of God
exhorting his people in the book of Leviticus 19:33–34 to take
special care of the alien in their midst, to treat such as one of their

---

[53] Robert W Funk, Roy W Hoover and The Jesus Seminar, Polebridge Press, 1998
p. 147.

own (that's a breaking down of ethnic barriers). We read of the prophets writing, 'What does the Lord require of you? To act justly, and to love mercy.' (Micah 6) 'Return to the Lord your God, for he is gracious and compassionate, slow to anger and abounding in love, and he relents from sending calamity.' (Psalm 103:8, Nehemiah 9:17, Exodus 32:14).

When we come to the New Testament and the records of the ministry of Jesus, how can one fathom the harsh sayings of Jesus, unless the view is taken that anything that is recorded of him which is not consistent with his view of love, to the extent of his even loving his enemies, surely cannot be of him?

This then I would maintain is the measuring line by which we interpret scripture, and indeed by which we are challenged and encouraged to live our lives. Though not able to reach the heights of Christ's love, we can reach out to it.

It is also through the spectacles of this love that we view the religions and philosophies of our world.

> 'Being loved' is something that happens to someone else. Loving is what happens to you. Without it and the desire that always goes with it makes gifts of love empty; life is maimed, mutilated, deprived, depraved. Without it, life is soured at source. With it, anything can be borne. To live without being loved is sorrowful. Without loving there is no real life.

(Jessamyn West, To see the Dream, Hodder & Stoughton Ltd, 1958, p.142.)

> Existence will remain meaningless for you if you yourself do not penetrate into it with active love, and if you do not in this way discover its meaning for yourself. Everything is waiting to be hallowed by you; it is waiting for this meaning to be disclosed and to be realised by you... Meet the world with the fullness of your being and you shall meet God. If you wish to believe, love!

(Martin Buber, in *Encounter with Martin Buber*, Aubrey Hodes, Allen Lane, The Penguin Press, 1972, p.66).[54]

---

[54] Quoted by William, Sykes in *Visions of Love*, Bible Reading Fellowship, 1992, p. 152.

At this juncture I believe it to be important to unravel what, according to Christian scripture, I believe, can be understood by the word 'God'. In John's Gospel, Chapter Four, verse twenty-four we read, 'God is spirit.' To discover what this spirit is we turn to 1 John 4:8: 'God is love,' and in verse 16 'God is love' is repeated. So in relation to understanding the word 'God' we have 'God' = Spirit (John 4:24) and Spirit = Love (1 John 4:8, and 16). In this first letter to John what can we say constitutes responding to God, to Christ? What is salvation?

In verse fifteen we read, 'If anyone acknowledges that Jesus is the son of God, God lives in him and he in God.' And so we know and rely on the love God has for us and then to acknowledge Jesus is to acknowledge the love he manifests.. In verse sixteen we read, 'Whoever lives in love lives in God, and God in him.' In verse twelve, 'No one has ever seen God; but if we love one another, God lives in us and his love is made complete in us.' How is this love manifest? It is God's love for us manifest in Christ. Verse ten: 'This is love; not that we loved God, but that he loved us and sent his son as an atoning sacrifice for our sins. Dear friends, since God so loved us, we also ought to love one another.' This love is a paradox, for it is vulnerable and it is powerful. In the cross we see just how vulnerable; and in this vulnerability, we see the power of love over hate and death.

In the cross the world receives what it does not deserve, forgiveness and mercy. Since we have received this we should also show forgiveness and mercy. 'God first loved us.' We were born in the image of this love, Genesis 1:26. Thus we are meant to love, to live in and for love. The power of love is its ability to give life even in death – love gives resurrection.

It is God's love for us that saves us, as we have already noted (John 4:10). It is not our works or even our faith but his sovereign love. Love for God is seen in attitude. Evidence of the spirit being in a person is in their attitudes, i.e. love for others in down-to-earth terms, as we have it in Matthew 25:34–36, when love is expressed to the sick, the prisoner, the stranger, the thirsty, the hungry, etc. The people doing this do not know they are doing it for Christ, they say they don't know him; none the less Christ informs them that because they were showing love for others they were responding to him, they were doing his work, they were accepting Christ – for they were accepting his love into their lives and living it. In 1 John 21 we read, 'Whoever loves God must love his brother also.' We do this in understanding, in fairness, in mercy, in forgiveness, in learning and giving faith and hope.

In 1 John, it could be seen that there is more than one qualification for love being in a person: (1) anyone who acknowledges Jesus as the son of God; and (2) anyone who lives in love. Or they can be seen as two sides of the same coin. Jesus came from, out of creative love, the energy that is the source of all life (God) = love. The terms son and father in relation to son of God and the heavenly father are terms (in an ideal understanding of father and son) of intimacy, terms which convey to us a God who is personal. Earthly terms are used to convey this. So to acknowledge Christ is to acknowledge love, and live it, which is what it seems Christ wishes to convey to those who were showing love in Matthew 25, in benevolent acts.

When we read in 1 John 4:19, 'We love because he first loved us,' we can say we were created out of his love, children of love, discovering this love is discovering our spiritual roots and our eternity of being ('for love is eternal', 1 Cor. 13:13), it remains, with faith and hope, but is greater than both, greater than all,.

When we read in the scriptures Jesus saying, 'I am the way, the truth and the life, no one comes to the father but by me,' in the light of what we have been looking at, we can say, 'the way, the truth and the life' is the love by which we come home to our spiritual roots to the creative energy of life, in personal terms to a heavenly father. To put it another way, to a source of energy which is love, which is intimate and personal, and this way is through the embodiment of the spirit of God, in the flesh. Jesus, recognised as such or not, is responded to, coming through to the father because of coming through manifestations of the love Christ is.

In this work we look at scripture through the sieve of this love, and consider Christian theology in the light of it.

Chapter 6: Searching Scripture – The Old Testament

For our encouragement in seeing the doctrine of the restoration of all things in the Old Testament we have the words of the apostle Peter. Speaking of the return of Jesus Christ he writes, 'The time comes for God to restore everything, as he promised long ago through his holy prophets...' (Acts 3:21). That anyone who does not listen to him (the Christ) will be cut off, verse 23. This is Peter quoting words attributed to Moses, at a time when the nation of Israel was being formed, and nationalistic feelings would be running high; but we note Peter goes on to remind his readers of still other Old Testament passages which imply that no one will in fact be cut off. He draws attention to Genesis 22:18, 26:4. 'He said to Abraham, "Through your offspring all peoples on earth will be blessed,"'

We note that when Peter speaks of the restitution of all things he informs us this was the message of the prophets – he would restore all things as 'he promised long ago through his holy prophets'.

The theme of restoration begins in Genesis, where we read humanity is made in the image of God: 'Then God said, let us make man in our own image' (1:26). That is, spirit; human beings are also spiritual beings, as well as bundles of chemicals. These, though wonderful, are yet not as incredible as humanity having spiritual roots. These roots are born of the Spirit who is love; that which gives life and light, which is truly everlasting.

It has been said the opening chapters of Genesis 'give to us the largest views of the loving sovereignty of God; and of the divine origin and destiny of mankind',[55] humanity coming from God returns to God (Romans 11:36: 'For from him and through him and to him are all things. To him be glory forever! Amen'). So it can be said that the divine plan to restore all humanity and all

---

[55] Westcott, *Revelation of the Father*, MacMillan, 1887.

creation is the central theme and unity of the Bible, and Westcott sees the true meaning of Judaism in the blessing of all nations. 'Its work was for humanity, the idea of Judaism is seen not in the covenant of Sinai, but in the covenant with Abraham.'[56]

In Genesis Chapter One, at the precise moment of what has been called the 'Fall' (humanity's spiritual decline beginning here) there is a promise that evil will be ultimately destroyed. In the language of myth (poetic language to convey a truth) a picture is painted of this promise, where evil as pictured in the serpent is destroyed, the serpent's head, the very peak, the root of evil will be crushed: 'I will put enmity between you and the woman, and between your offspring and hers; he will crush your head, and you will strike his heel.'

We note the promise is not of the serpent merely being wounded, but of a fatal wound. It is worthy of note, as Allin points out,

> …That even those who take extreme views of future punishment seem to agree in the belief that Adam and Eve found mercy. But, if so, it may well be asked – shall they who were the authors of the Fall, and all its woe, escape? Shall they who, created upright, fall – yet find mercy at the last, while so many involuntary inheritors of a fallen nature are doomed?[57]

Thus mercy can be seen in the very first book of the Bible as it has come down to us. Restoration of all things in the promise to Abraham, and the destruction of evil ultimately and finally.

As regards the covenant to Abraham, a promise that all the nations of the world would be blessed, there are intimations of this universal blessing in the Law, the Psalms and the Prophets. In the Law a fundamental ingredient was the institution of the 'first-born' and the 'first fruits'. The 'first fruits' pledge all the harvest and the 'first born' the whole family. So we can say the chosen people of God (i.e. the elect 'Israel is my son, my first born') are the channels through which the whole world will be blessed, so we have repeated promises to Abraham.

---

[56] Ibid.

[57] *Universalism Asserted*, p. 211, note.

A sheaf of wheat or the 'first fruits' presented to the Lord was a consecrating and pledging of the whole harvest; all the 'first-born' of flocks and herds were the Lord's. This was an acknowledgement, a pledge, that all were his. Here we notice that Jesus Christ is spoken of as the 'first fruits' (1 Corinthians 15:23). The context actually implies – no, not implies, but explicitly states – that 'as in Adam all die, so in Christ all will be made alive...' (verse 22).

When we come to the Psalms we have again a universal theme revealed. Psalm 22:27: 'All the ends of the earth will remember and turn to the Lord, and all the families of the nations will bow down before him.' And it will not do for some to say such verses talk of nations having no choice, and are thus compelled; this verse refers to a turning to the Lord and then a bowing before him. And what message would it convey if it were an enforced dominion? It would be no better than what the dictators of the world have done, which is contrary to God, the creator Spirit, love.

There are many Psalms which speak of all the nations rejoicing in the sovereignty of God. All nations shall come and worship: 'All the earth bows down to you; they sing praise to you, they sing praise to your name' (Psalm 66:4); 'All kings will bow down to him and all nations will serve him' (Psalm 72:11). Psalm after Psalm could be quoted on this theme. The whole earth is not lamenting that it is having to bow down in homage, but rejoicing, delighting in doing so.

It is a bowing, doing homage to the fragility of love, that creates. Vulnerable, yet powerful, its power is seen in fragmented weakness, as on the cross; it is the light that John speaks of in the prologue to his Gospel, that has not been understood, that has never been put out; it cannot be put out. It is the breath of God, Spirit, breathing out that love that is a mystery and wonder we cannot comprehend, which will ultimately do away with evil and the negative forces in the world, not by the world's understanding of power, but a power that is seen in apparent weakness: Maximillian Kolbe in a concentration camp, who none the less to dying and hopeless people brings the light of eternal life, which is everlasting love... the love seen in a Gladys Aylward, a small, weak, frail-looking woman, who in the love of Christ saves the children she rescues from the streets. One could go on and on with examples of this Spirit, this love, this God living in the lives of people in this world. The supreme weakness is Christ on a cross – bringing eternal everlasting hope and salvation for the world.

The Psalms rejoice in this love, this spirit that constructs, that creates, that brings life and hope and blessing. When we turn to the Prophets we see again the silver lining of universal salvation. In Isaiah 54 we get the contrast between God's anger and his compassion, his mercy: '"In a surge of anger I hid my face from you for a moment, but with everlasting kindness I will have compassion on you," says the Lord your redeemer.'

Will the Lord, whose anger lasts but for a moment, in any way be glorified in his anger everlastingly poured out on a people who are in a hell? There is no logic in such a notion; it is a contradiction of the worst kind.

Turning to the Prophets we read in Isaiah words from Jehovah: 'Turn to me and be saved, all the ends of the earth; for I am God and there is no other. By myself I have sworn, my mouth has uttered in all integrity a word that will not be revoked. Before me every knee will bow; by me every tongue will swear. They will say of me, "In the Lord alone are righteousness and strength."' (Isaiah 45:23)

Every tongue will take an oath of loyalty to him? This could well be deduced from this passage; and can we not also deduce that since this is attributed as coming from the mouth of God, he will accomplish his purpose, for his word will not be revoked; and from Genesis we understand that when God spoke it happened: 'and God said let there be light and there was light'. In Hebrew understanding, the word was action. And in Job 42:2 we read of God that, 'no plan of yours can be thwarted'.

In Isaiah 53:11 we read, 'After the suffering (AV 'travail') of his soul, he will see the light of life and be satisfied.' Commenting on this verse, Allin asks:

By what ingenuity can hopeless, endless evil be reconciled with these words? How can I accept a creed that asks me to believe that Christ is satisfied, while his own children are given over to endless ruin. Who believes this of Jesus Christ? Who can believe him 'satisfied' with the final and utter ruin of any one soul for whom he died? – 'satisfied' that his cross should fail? – 'satisfied' with the victory of evil, in so much as a solitary case?[58]

The Psalms and the Prophets again and again draw our attention to the vastness of God's mercy. Even when we turn to Lamentations, we read in 3:31–32: 'For men are not cast off from the Lord for ever, though he brings grief, he will show compassion, so great is his unfailing love'.

And again we see in Isaiah 57:16: 'I will not accuse forever, nor will I always be angry, for then the spirit of man would grow faint before me – the breath of man that I have created.' How then can God's wrath be continually vented on those in hell? In Jeremiah 3:12 we read, 'I am merciful,' declares the Lord, 'I will not be angry forever.' The phrase, 'his love (or mercy) endures forever', is a statement that is repeated no less than twenty-six times in just one Psalm, Psalm 136, which in the NIV is translated, 'His love endures for ever'. In the Prophet Micah we read in 7:18: '…you do not stay angry forever but delight to show mercy…'

Now if we accept this, what becomes of the doctrine of everlasting punishment, or indeed of annihilation, both being seen as eternal punishment? If God's anger is temporary, how is it possible for it to be endless?

It is sad to note that in Chris Morgan's book, *Jonathan Edwards and Hell*, wrath and judgment take precedence over love and mercy. He writes, '…it is not contrary to God's love to limit the period of mercy, to execute penal justice, or to allow suffering.'[59] Now this does not sit well with such scriptures as we have looked at, such scriptures as Lamentations 3:22, '…because of the Lord's great love we are not consumed, for his compassions never fail'. In the RSV, this reads as 'the steadfast love of the Lord never ceases, his mercies never come to an end'.

In the Prophet Daniel 7:14, we read of the 'son of man' (a favourite title of Jesus) having universal authority and having a

---

[58] *Universalism Asserted*, Published by Williams and Norgate, 1895.
[59] Jonathan Edwards as quoted in *Jonathan Edwards and Hell*, Mentor Books, 2004 p.132.

kingdom that will never be destroyed: 'He was given authority, glory and sovereign power; all peoples, nations and men of every language worshipped him. His dominion is an everlasting dominion that will not pass away, and his kingdom is one that will never be destroyed.'

Among the minor Prophets, in Joel 2:28 we read of the spirit being poured out on all flesh. In Habakkuk, looking beyond judgement sees the earth filled with the knowledge and glory of the Lord as the waters cover the sea; all the minor Prophets see judgement followed by a world redeemed to the love and the service of righteousness. Maybe we can enter into the ethos of Peter's words at the birth of the church as he proclaims the vast and glorious scope of universal restoration, of all things made new, 'as he promised long ago through his holy prophets...' (Acts 3:21).

We do recognise that those who hold to the doctrine of ever-lasting punishment turn to certain Old Testament passages for support, so we now turn our attention to some of the most significant.

In Isaiah 33:14 we read: 'The sinners in Zion are terrified; trembling grips the godless: who of us can dwell with consuming fire? Who of us can dwell with everlasting burning?' This text was sadly misapplied by Jonathan Edwards; to apply it to eternal punishment is to tear it from its context. The prophet is speaking of the horrors of the Assyrian invasion. The words apply to a temporal event. Who will be able to stand against the Assyrian onslaught? Who can stand against this Assyrian constant burning (will it ever stop)? is the feeling of the unrighteous in the face of this terrifying Assyrian invasion; it has nothing to do with ever-lasting punishment.

Another passage is Isaiah 66:24: 'And they will go out and look upon the dead bodies of those who rebelled against me; their worm will not die, nor will their fire be quenched, and they will be loathsome to all mankind.'

It has to be noted first that these verses are omitted by the best manuscripts. However, let us look at these verses in context. The prophet is speaking of Jerusalem and its future peace and of the retribution to come on all idolaters, apostates, and those who eat swine's flesh and other abominations, and the nations shall come and look on the abhorrent valley which is full of rotting corpses. There is nothing in this passage about everlasting punishment. Farrar observes:

> To give it such an explanation is to read Isaiah as if he were writing in the style of Thomas Aquinas, and to turn Semitic Passion into theological prose. Even if, in full violation of all the Laws of Eastern Idiom and Poetry, we were to be so unreasonable as to understand literal worms that literally do not die, and fires literally unquenchable – a proceeding that nothing could excuse but a sort of idolatry of words and syllables – how can carcases and dead corpses feel the gnawing of the worm, or the burning of the flame? Are we to torture the text into a doctrine of horror by understanding metaphorically the word which is obviously literal, and by understanding literally (so far as it suits us) the expressions which are obviously metaphorical? The poet in his burning patriotism is only depicting in bold imagery the triumph of his people, and the special mention of new moons and Sabbaths, and pilgrimages to a spot outside Jerusalem, as well as the fact that he is speaking of dead corpses, should alone have sufficed to rescue his passionate metaphors from being abused into an endless eschatology.[60]

Jan Bonda, commenting on this verse, asks:

> Does this final passage of the book crush the hope for all people that is proclaimed in the book of Isaiah? The great feast for all nations, the annihilation of death and the wiping away of all tears (25:6–8); the joyful message that all flesh will see God's redemption (40:5); that every knee shall bow before God and praise him (45:23) – will all this be cancelled? If that were so, these words would not have been included in this book![61]

Yet another passage referred to is found in Daniel 12:2: 'Multitudes that sleep in the dust of the earth will awake: some to everlasting life, others to shame and everlasting contempt.'

It has to be admitted that the translation of this verse is

---

[60] *Mercy and Judgement*, pp. 441–442.
[61] *The One Purpose of God*, pp. 216–217.

uncertain, in fact some would say far too uncertain to be relied upon. It is not easy to see the particular disaster that the prophet is referring to. However the hub of the matter is to be found in the translation of the Hebrew word *olam*. Its proper meaning is 'an age', an indefinite period, long or short. Sadly it has confusingly been translated into English as 'everlasting' or 'eternal'. Jan Bonda reminds us that the use of the word 'eternal' in the context of the giving of the Mosaic law indicates that it does not mean endless. About thirty times we read about an 'eternal', 'perpetual', 'ordinance', but they were not everlasting. And as F W Farrar observes:

The phrases which are asserted to imply endlessness are again and again used of things which have long since ceased to be. If olam meant 'eternity', how came it to have a plural (a olamim)? and how came the Jews to talk of 'for ever and beyond'? The latter expression alone was decisive to the clear mind of Origen. He says that the authority of Holy Scripture taught him that the word rendered 'eternity' meant 'limited duration'.

Since aion meant 'an age', aionios means properly 'belonging to an age', or 'age long'; and anyone who asserts that it must always mean 'endless' defends a position which even Augustine practically abandoned twelve centuries ago. Even if aion always meant 'eternity' – which is not the case either in classic or Hellenistic Greek – aionios could still only mean 'belonging to eternity', not 'lasting through it'. Aionios does not even mean 'endless within the sphere of its own existence'. For in Deut. xxiii.3 'for ever' is distinctly made an equivalent to 'even to their tenth generation'. So again is Isaiah 1x.15, 'I will make thee an aeonian Excellency,' is explained in the next clause by 'a joy of many generations'; and in Lamentations 5:19 'for ever and ever' is the equivalent of 'from generation to generation'...

The word by itself – whether adjective or substantive – never means endless. If such were its meaning, or that of its Hebrew equivalent, the Jews would have been perfectly justified in rejecting the Christian religion which proclaimed the annulment of ordinances which in their law they had again and again been told were to be 'eternal' and 'for ever'. If they could have established that meaning of the word they would have had an unanswerable argument against Christianity. Aionios may in some instances connote endlessness, because it catches something of its colour from the words to which it is joined; just as the word 'indefinite' might catch the sense of 'infinite' if, in speaking of things which for other reasons I knew to be 'infinite in duration'. It is a word which, like many other adjectives, shines simply 'by reflected light'.62

It is interesting to note that even someone like Leontius of Byzantium in arguing against Universalists actually has to admit that aion is used of a definite period.

It is therefore important to see the whole ethos of scripture on any particular subject, to look at the evidence against the whole biblical background, as we have endeavoured to do.

The horrors of everlasting punishment crumble in the face of overwhelming evidence from the original languages of both the Old and New Testaments.

Again and again, restoration takes place in the history of Israel, and the hope of salvation is held out again and again to the people. Farrar points out that if the teaching concerning 'everlasting punishment' were so crucial, then surely it would have been made more explicit in the Old Testament, when one considers it constitutes the peculiar message of God to man during some four millenniums of human history.63

Thus if this teaching on 'hell' were so crucial, as the exponents of everlasting punishment would have us believe, and essential for all humanity to know, then surely the divine spirit would have made sure it was included in the teaching of Israel's religious history, as righteousness, punishment for wrong, mercy and restoration are constantly repeated.

There are many passages in the Old Testament which speak of the mercy of God. We do not deny there are passages of judgement and punishment, but as I have sought to show these are never the last word. F W Farrar comments:

---

62 *Mercy and Judgement*, pp. 378–379.

63 *Mercy and Judgement*, p.435. Farrar expands on his point thus: Now it is not pretended by anyone that the Jews or the Pagans of those ages were less immortal than we, or that their future was a different one from ours. And if so, surely the popular doctrine of hell, were it a true one, was one which, on the repeated assertions of its advocates, it infinitely important for man to know. And it would indeed have required very explicit teaching – teaching infinitely stronger than the attempt to put a new and literal meaning into a Hebrew phrase which simply implied 'the hidden' and 'the indefinite'.

…Whether we turn to the Old Testament or the New Testament, there is an overwhelming mass of evidence on the side of those who think that God's highest glory is the prerogative of absolute and boundless mercy – that in the words of our collect 'his nature and property are ever to have mercy and forgive.' If we are to press to the utmost limits the meaning of the expression 'for ever' and 'eternal' in the half-dozen texts scattered throughout the Bible which seem at first sight to reveal for all sinners a hopeless and endless doom at the moment of death, are we to ignore, or minimize or explain away the multitudes of such texts as these?:- And the Lord passed by before him, and proclaimed, the Eternal, the Eternal, a God merciful and gracious, long-suffering and abundant in goodness and truth, keeping mercy for thousands, forgiving iniquity and transgression and sin, but who will by no means always leave unpunished. – Exodus 34:6, 7. (Punishment, yes – not eternal, but remedial).

His anger endureth but a moment; in His favour is mercy. – Psalm 30:5.

Good and upright is the Lord: therefore will He teach sinners in the way. – Psalm 25:8.

Judgement is to put right what is wrong, to 'teach sinners the way'.

If the Lord will not retain his anger for eternity, how could it be possible for some to still be under his anger in hell for ever? The Old Testament's emphasis is on salvation for mankind, not destruction, and as we shall see this is also the message of the New Testament.

Chapter 7: Searching the Scripture – The New Testament

What does the teaching of eternal punishment in hell, everlasting torment, require with regard to scripture?

> It practically requires a MUTILATED BIBLE. And more than this, it bids us expunge precisely that which is noblest and divinest in Holy Scripture...

Allen then informs us that Scripture's essential purpose

> is to unfold His name, who is 'Our Father', and to proclaim His full victory in the extinction of all evil, and not its perpetuation in hell. I protest against teaching that 'all' means in scriptural phrase absolutely 'all' when some evil is foretold, but that 'all' means only 'some' when spoken of final salvation.
>
> So rooted is this most inequitable mode of interpretation, that it has become involuntary. The restitution of all things means, we are told, that only some beings are to be restored, while some are tortured forever, or annihilated. That God shall be finally 'All in All' means that he will shut up many forever in endless evil, to blaspheme and hate him eternally, and only save the rest. That his tender mercies are over all his works means, in the ordinary creed, that his tender mercies expire at the gates of hell. Solemn as is the question, there is something almost ludicrous, when we find those who so teach, then turning round to charge us with evading the words of scripture. I submit the entire history of exegesis contains no stronger fact than this persistent ignoring of so large a part of the New Testament.[64]

Allin then lists texts after texts which are closely linked together, commencing at creation, 'when all things were created by Christ,

---

[64] T Allin, *Universalism Asserted*, on the Authority of Reason the Fathers and Holy Scripture, Williams & Norgate, 1895, p. 221.

who, therefore, as Saint Paul implies, reconciles (in fact re-creates) all things unto God – Col. 1:16:20'. Hence his work is the restitution of all things. Allin makes the point this is not just a random list piled up anyhow, he writes: 'They are the expression of that purpose which runs through the Bible, a purpose first stated in man's creation in God's image, a purpose to be traced in the Law, the Psalms and Prophets, and most clearly in the New Testament'.[65]

When we read in Matthew 18:11 that 'the son of man came to save what was lost', the question is, will he accomplish this task, or will he fail? We read in 1 Corinthians 13:8 how 'Love never fails'; we read that it 'always perseveres', in verse 7. The words 'the son of man came to save what was lost' are followed up with the parable of the lost sheep indicating that even if all but one is safe the shepherd will go after that one, and bring it back so that they are all safe in the fold. Even though some manuscripts exclude the introductory words to this parable, i.e. 'the son of man came to save what was lost', the parable itself says it all. And as Allin asks, 'How can the lost be saved, if some are left unsaved?'

In Matthew 19:28, we read of Jesus speaking about the renewal of all things. This passage speaks of universal restoration, and it is interesting to note it is in the context of judgement; judgement is not just about punishment for wrongdoing, but about putting right that which is wrong in order to bring restitution.

In 2 Corinthians 5:19 we read: 'God was reconciling the world to himself in Christ, not counting men's sins against them.' Are we to suppose God is not able to do this? In Galatians 3:8 we read that to Abraham was given this promise, 'All nations will be blessed through you.' In Ephesians 1:10 we read: '...when the times will have reached their fulfilment to bring all things in heaven and on earth together under one head even Christ'. This certainly points to the whole universe being blessed; if some were left unblessed, it would not be the whole universe.

In Colossians 1:15–20 we read that all things in heaven and on earth, visible and invisible, will be reconciled through Christ's

---

[65] Ibid., pp. 221–224.

sacrifice (verse 20). This again points to a universal salvation, it even implies the reconciliation of the microscopic world, the whole of nature being renewed.

In 1 Timothy 4:10 we read: '...we have put our hope in the living God, who is the saviour of all men, and especially of those who believe'. Here we have the clear statement that God is the saviour of all people as well as those who believe, which seems to imply that those who believe are saved and become the vehicles by which all are saved. This could possibly be referring to the Jewish people – 'those who believe' – in which case the same point applies; one could go on to affirm that there is therefore an 'elect' through which all are saved.

In 2 Timothy 1:10 we read: 'It has now been revealed through the appearing of our saviour, Jesus Christ, who has destroyed death and has brought life and immortality to light through the gospel, and of this gospel I was appointed a herald and an apostle and a teacher.' T Allin has commented on this passage:

For death abolished, and yet death in its worst form, the second death,[66] maintained for ever, are plain contradictions. Will those who maintain the doctrine of conditional immortality explain how death can be abolished, and yet swallow up finally all sinners in a sentence of annihilation?[67]

In Hebrews 2:14–15, speaking of Jesus Paul says: 'Since the children have flesh and blood, he too shared in their humanity so that by his death he might destroy him who holds the power of death – that is the devil – and free those who all their lives were held in slavery by their fear of death.'

It is obvious that the destruction of the devil, symbolic of all that is evil, destructive and of death, is inconsistent with the continuance of evil eternally. It surely informs us that there will come a time when all evil, all distortion in humanity and in nature, all evil elements in the world will at last come to an end.

We read in 1 Corinthians 13 that love never ends, and as we have noted it never fails, it is impossible on this premise for a hell to exist for ever, or for death to be the end; and if it is impossible

---

[66] 'Then death and Hades were thrown into the lake of fire...' Revelation 20:14
[67] Allin, p. 245.

for this love to condemn anyone to eternal torture, how can God who is referred to as a 'heavenly Father' condemn any of his children to this?

Now all this does not imply that evil will go unpunished, that all wrong is brushed under the carpet. There is a time when justice will be done, for it is clear it is not always done in this world. There are those, as has been observed, who pour out their lives in compassion for others, who themselves suffer much, ill health, poverty, etc.; and there are those who live lives of luxury and who abuse others on the way to worldly wealth, power and prestige. So judgement, if not in this life, is spoken of as taking place in the next. However, as already observed, judgement, while including punishment, is concerned above all with putting right that which is wrong – restoration – otherwise there is no point in it.

In the epistle to the Hebrews the illustration is given of a parent who punishes their child, not in vindictiveness, but desiring that the child develops into a responsible caring person, 12:9–13:

> We have all had fathers [obviously speaking of good fathers] who disciplined us and we respected them for it. How much more should we submit to our spiritual father and live! Our fathers disciplined us for a little while as they thought best; but God dis-ciplines us for our good… therefore, strengthen your feeble arms and weak knees. Make level paths for your feet, so that the lame may not be disabled, but rather healed.

Here we are looking at remedial punishment, issuing forth in wholeness and healing. Universal salvation does not make light of wrongdoing. Allin writes, 'I earnestly assert the punishment of sin (awful it may well be, in its duration and nature for the hardened offender) but in all cases directed by love and justice to the final extirpation of evil'[68] – thus the final salvation of the sinner.

> In the light of Calvary it is that we are bound to see the guilt of sin. But let us beware, lest, as we stand in thought by the cross, we virtually dishonour the atonement by limiting its power to save – by teaching men that Christ is after all vanquished… for he

---

[68] Ibid., p. 249.

never said, 'I if I be lifted up, will draw some men', or even 'most men', but 'I WILL DRAW ALL MEN UNTO ME'.[69]

Then we have the famous passage in Luke 6:27–35 about loving our enemies, doing good to those who hate us. Now, how can endless punishment be reconciled with the spirit of this text? If, as orthodox Christian teaching accepts, Jesus is the embodiment of God, how can God tell us to love our enemies and do good to those who hate us, while at the same time he means to punish for ever those who wrong him?

In the world, human beings have no particular problem in understanding retribution in terms of vengeance, the destruction of the enemy; it happens all the time. What is phenomenal is that one should seek the very best for an enemy, which is what love will do. Loving one's enemies is the very miracle of our salvation. Jesus Christ preached this, and died proving it. The values of the kingdom of heaven turn the world's values on their heads. The opposite of revenge and destruction is love, justice, reconciliation and salvation.

Thank God the values of the kingdom have been put into practice, and when they have remarkable things happen. Nelson Mandela, after twenty seven years in prison, coming out of confinement with the potential power to take revenge on all those who put him there, on all those who had committed crimes against the black population, set up a 'truth and reconciliation commission'. Its purpose, as the name suggests, was to bring the population of the country together, forgiving the past, building a future of mutual trust and understanding, learning a new way of living together in peace. His comment to his critics was 'This country needs mercy more than it needs justice.'

The New Testament teaching that places love above hate (that is in stark contrast to the teaching of punishing an enemy for ever in a torture chamber that has been given the name 'hell') has a very down-to-earth application. While refuting the doctrine of hell may for many be totally irrelevant (for they don't believe in it anyway, it is so absurd), none the less it has a great deal to say

---

[69] Ibid., p. 250.

regarding the hells we can create for one another on earth.

Nelson Mandela brought a bit of heaven down to earth, to coin a phrase, when he set up his truth and reconciliation commission. The New Testament teaching on love put into practice would prevent many of the hells humanity creates for itself on earth, between nations, within nations, within communities, between individuals. The message of salvation in the New Testament is about building up, not knocking down. It's about living life to the full, not destroying or maiming life for ever. Jesus spoke of bringing abundant life; temporal life and eternal life, life lived now and everlasting life. At the commencement of his ministry, the first recorded sermon we have of Jesus was when he preached in the synagogue in Nazareth from the prophet Isaiah, ascribing the message to his own ministry, he said this scripture was fulfilled in him,

'The spirit of the Lord is on me, because he has anointed me to preach good news to the poor. He has sent me to proclaim freedom for the prisoners, and recovery of sight for the blind, to release the oppressed, to proclaim the year of the Lord's favour.'

His message to John the Baptist, who was in prison and having doubts about Jesus, was to tell John's disciples, 'Go back and report to John what you have seen and heard: the blind receive sight, the lame walk, those who have leprosy are cured, the deaf hear, the dead are raised, the good news is preached to the poor.' (Matthew 11: 4–5)

It is a message of construction not destruction, it's Gospel, it's good news!

Whenever there are any sayings attributed to Jesus that do not fit in with his words to love enemies and neighbours and oneself, his actions in healings of mind, body and spirit, they cannot be of him.

It is a fact that in literature and in the news media, time and time again words are reported to come from celebrities, but when the people in question are asked about them, it is discovered they never spoke these words, or they were misinterpreted. A person is judged by their whole input into society, and Jesus Christ's whole ministry is overflowingly seen in forgiveness and love, encouraging people to have a right about-turn in their attitudes, in the direction of love, in word and deed (called repentance).

> The problem with the concept of a severely punishing God is that there seems to be no room allowed for our natural infirmities[70] …it is quite possible that an uncharitable person had no charity shown to them during their childhood, which may have been unspeakably vile. While this thought does not justify their uncharitable attitude to their fellow creatures, it ought at least to modify the judgement given at the end of the day. Any judge sentencing a criminal first finds out the circumstances of the person before pronouncing the sentence. One would hope at least as much from God, all of whose creatures have defects of one type or another, as part of their learning and growth into full personhood. The cruelly punitive God preached in some revivalistic rallies may shock rather unhappy, guilt-ridden people into 'declaring for Christ', but this God offends the sensitivity of more discerning listeners, who feel, possibly rightly, that they can do without such a being in their lives.[71]

The punitive God, the God of punishment, is not the God that Jesus Christ embodies and proclaims when he encourages us to love ourselves, our neighbours and even our enemies! or a love that will ultimately conquer hate, destruction and death. It is of course crucial that we look at passages in the New Testament which use phrases such as 'eternal punishment'. To such passages we shall turn our attention; what is also crucial, however, is to explore the meaning of the word used in the New Testament which has given rise to the understanding of punishment as everlasting.

There are many adjectives and phrases that the Lord Jesus Christ and the apostles could have used to convey the idea of 'everlasting', and 'endlessness' easily and simply in Hebrew or Greek in a hundred different and indisputable ways; but not one of these most decisive adjectives, not one of these indisputable phrases, is even once applied to Hades or Gehenna.

There are two very straight forward adverbs in the New Testament, any one of which would have been regarded as

---

[70] Referring to the story of the Last Judgement as recorded in Matthew 25.
[71] Martin Israel, *Life Eternal*, SPCK, 1993, pp. 48–49.

decisive. One is *aei* (always). It occurs eight times in the New Testament, but not once in relation to future punishment. The other is *pantote*, which also occurs eight times, but never of future punishment!

The strong phrase 'to the uttermost' (*eis to panteles*) found in Hebrews 7:25, AV, (NIV – 'completely') occurs once in the New Testament. It is applied to salvation, not condemnation, again the strong phrase, 'for perpetuity' AV (NIV 'for all time') – (*eis to dienekes*) occurs twice in the New Testament, Hebrews 10:12 and in 10:14, of God and of final sanctification, it is never ever used of future punishment.

In the New Testament we are told that the glory of Christ shall last 'to all generations' (*eis pantas tous aiōnas* – *eis pantas tous*). Farrar comments, 'had such an expression been applied even so much as once to the dominion of evil, it would have been regarded as decisive, but it is not so applied, not even by Jude.'[72]

And Farrar informs us that in Hebrew the expression *leolam vaed* (for ever and beyond) occurs some fifteen times in the Old Testament, and even then in a perfectly general sense, but it is never used for future punishment!

It seems clear that the Old Testament which Jesus, the disciples and the Jewish people of his day knew would not have understood Gehenna and Hades, as meaning 'everlasting'; that is why it is such a tragedy that it has been translated this way in English.

The whole ethos of scripture is God seeking to bring humanity right through to salvation, as we have already noted the parable of the good shepherd shows this so clearly. Even though all are gathered safely in save one, the good shepherd goes out to find that one, and in Luke's account succeeds in doing so. In order that all are safely gathered in, to emphasise this, the Lord Jesus gives these three parables in Luke 15: the lost sheep, the lost coin, and the lost son. And we note in the story of the lost son, even the son who was bitter because he was hurt is welcomed into the house that all may be united as one family. He says to this son, 'My son, everything that I have is yours. But we had to celebrate and be

---

[72] *Mercy and Judgement*, p. 388. Jude 25 can also be translated 'before all generations'.

glad, because this brother of yours was dead and is alive again, he was lost and is found.' (Luke 15:31–32).

Jesus is even including in the household of God those religious leaders who gave him so much trouble, and who would eventually plot to kill him; he even includes those who are so critical of his ministry, for this parable and the others in this chapter are directed to them (Luke 15:1–3). Christ is in the business of reconciliation so that the family of man is one in his kingdom. It is significant that in the parable of the lost son, where the older son is so critical of the father for welcoming back the son who has been such a sinner, the father welcomes this critical son into the home as well. Christ, in return for the criticism he has received from the Pharisees and teachers of the Law, includes them in the family home of the Spirit – even, it seems, before they show signs of repentance. He returns goodness and love for bitterness!

At this point I will quote extensively from Jan Bonda who emphasises that the death of Christ is the salvation of the many, in fact the whole world. He does this by facing head-on texts in the Old Testament, as being the Bible Jesus knew. We have already seen how the word *aionios*, once recognised for what it is, throws a completely new light on Matthew 25:46. As Farrar puts it, 'When the true meaning of the word "aeonian" is restored, the passages ceases entirely to prove the doctrine of endless torments.'

But Bonda opens up still yet another shaft of light on this passage as follows:

Someone who thinks that in Matthew 25:46 Jesus announces the end of the history of the world as an outcome we simply have to accept, acts as if the entire history of Jesus' suffering and death does not affect the many who go to eternal punishment. What is happening here? It is what Moses was after when he put himself in the breach on behalf of disobedient Israel. 'If you will only forgive their sins – but if not, blot me out of the book that you have written' (Exodus 32:32). God did not blot Moses out of his book; but this is the way Christ must go – the way of being forsaken by God. 'How then would the scriptures be fulfilled, which say it must happen in this way?' (Matthew 26:54).

Jesus goes the way of the cross in order to open for these many the way of escape from eternal punishment; to make sure that their 'going away to eternal punishment' will be followed by their return. For that very reason he became obedient until death on the cross. Therefore, every knee shall bow, and every tongue shall at last confess: Jesus is Lord, to the glory of God the father (Phil. 2:8–11).

The Term 'Eternal' and God's Purpose

We now return to the term 'eternal'. In scripture, 'eternity' does not refer to a situation God wants to see continued without end. That the fire of God's wrath on Israel will burn eternally (Jeremiah 17:4), that God puts eternal shame, eternal contempt on Israel (18:40), does not indicate that this achieves God's ultimate purpose. On the contrary, as long as this state continues, it merely means that Israel is not yet what she should be. His purpose is, and remains, the return of his disobedient people to him, the making of a new covenant. Then, until all eternity, Jerusalem shall never again be uprooted or overthrown (31:31–40). Contrary to the everlasting nature of the punishment, there will be no end to the eternity of God's salvation. Why not? Because then Israel will fully answer to God's intentions; it has become the people of God that does his will with all its heart. That is God's one and only purpose for Israel. That is also the answer to the argument put forward by the church fathers Augustine and Chrysostom (I, 3), that the eternal punishment of Matthew 25:46 has to be endless, since otherwise it must be assumed that eternal life will also have an end. Eternal life continues, since it is God's purpose for humanity. Eternal punishment, however, does not forever continue, since that punishment itself is not his goal. When God's purpose has been achieved, there is no need for further punishment – for sin no longer exists!

Let us review. The word 'eternal' has played a major role in the doctrine of eternal punishment. But what scripture tells us about God's purpose with this punishment remained a secondary concern. We have seen that this divine purpose must be our first interest in any biblical discourse about the eternity of the punishment. Never is there any other purpose than that the unbeliever return to obedience to God. Nowhere in scripture do we find a statement that tells us that God wants those who are punished to suffer without end – that is not the purpose for which God created humans! If we keep this singular purpose of God in focus, we understand that eternal punishment is punishment that has as its only purpose an obedient return to the God of love.[73]

F W Farrar, commenting on Matthew 25, writes:

'Depart from Me, ye cursed, into aeonian fire …'

The words, therefore, denounce a stern judgment on those who are unmerciful and hard-hearted. That we are dealing with language which cannot be pressed into close details is manifest from the fact that the decision is represented as turning solely on the fulfilment or neglect of one single virtue – active benevolence. When the true meaning of the word 'aeōnian' is restored, the passage ceases entirely to prove the doctrine of 'endless torments', even if these other features of it did not exclude such an explanation.

But the scene described is not the judgment of the dead at all, but of the living. It is the trial of 'all the Gentiles' at the second coming of Christ. So little of certainty can there be in the details of its eschatology that such commentators as Keil, Olshausen, and Greswell confine its application to Gentiles only, whereas Grotius and Meyer confine it to Christians only. We cannot then assert with confidence that it is meant to shadow forth the ultimate doom of individual men, but the judgments and losses which follow on the exclusion from the kingdom of Christ. It is a description, based on Old Testament metaphors, of that which shall happen to those Gentiles who, at Christ's coming – His Parousia at the close of the old dispensation – shall be found rejecting Him and persecuting His children. The fire which burns for them is that fire which ever burns against sin, and which is therefore described as prepared for the devil and his angels. There is nothing to indicate that this 'fire of the age to come' may not cease when that age is merged into the great, the final, and the blessed consummation.

Further, our Lord could hardly have used the metaphor of the shepherd separating the sheep from the goats without direct

---

[73] *The One Purpose of God*, pp. 217–219.

reference to the thirty-fourth chapter of Ezekiel. In that chapter God, indignant with the idle and selfish shepherds, says, 'Behold I judge between cattle and cattle, between the rams and he-goats'; or perhaps rather 'between other cattle and the rams and the he-goats.' But the sheep and goats are alike clean; they alike form part of the common flock; and in the passage of Ezekiel are all under one loving shepherd, and the words used by our Lord for goats – 'eriphia' – literally 'kidlings' – has nothing itself which points to final exclusion or implacable indignation.[74]

Matthew 25:31–46 was the passage most confidently relied on by patristic writers, and by subsequent advocates of hell; and the chief text on which the doctrine of eternal damnation was built.

'And these shall go away into everlasting punishment but the righteous into life eternal,' as the AV diversely translates – aiōnios it was regarded, not as a similitude, but as a description of the actual days of judgement. Yet there are few passages in the Gospels that have been more challenged by modern critics, since the study of apocalypse began; for nearly every sentence can be traced to the Jewish apocalyptic books. We can indeed defend its genuineness, but only on the grounds that the parable of Jesus is here clothed – magnificently – in the phraseology with which the evangelist was familiar. We have only Matthew's version, and therefore have no means of checking it; but we can see him occupied as on other occasions in colouring the words of the master with the lurid tints which he loved. The originals have been found for most of the phrases. 'The fire prepared for the devil' and 'aeonian punishment' are commonplace of apocalyptic. 'The son of man coming in his glory', and 'sitting on the throne of his glory' are almost verbatim from the book of Enoch (45.3) (62.5), as is the description of the righteous sheep, and sinners as other animals (90). There is something gentler in Matthew's 'goats' for an eastern shepherd esteems his goats as much as his sheep, and indeed they look much alike. The whole picture had been already drawn in another apocalyptic book, *The Secrets of Enoch.*

'This place, O Enoch, is prepared for the righteous, who... give bread to the hungry, and cover the naked with clothing, and

---

[74] *Mercy and Judgement*, pp. 457–458.

raise up the fallen, and help injured orphans.'

And in the tenth chapter of this book an eternal inheritance of torment is prepared for those who 'being able to satisfy the empty, made the hungering to die; being able to clothe, stripped the naked'.

The idea of the Son of Man judging, and condemning to aeōnian torment those who have oppressed the poor is thus derived from other sources; 'The similitude's of Enoch' is the background, and it is a mistake to extract doctrine, as pointed out, from the setting which is presupposed and assumed. But two features are original. 1) The wicked are not merely those who have broken the law and oppressed the poor, but those who have failed to do good when they had the opportunity 2) Jesus identifies himself in a tender and splendid way with the outcast and poor. In as much as ye did it unto one of these my brethren, even the least, ye did it unto me.

'And these shall go away into eternal punishment', etc. This verse is probably added by Matthew and recalls Daniel 12:2.

Farrar makes it clear that all the horrible human inferences and imaginations which 'have for centuries been conglomerated into the meaning of "hell", but which hardly came into existence till the fifth century, …constitute such a belief as the church has never at any time required.'[75] Farrar informs us that as he interprets the texts he cannot forget the intensity of God's love for man.

'That love is not quenched by our sinfulness, but only mingled with grief.' He then draws attention to God's love for people declared in scripture, as a mother's yearning, a lover's agonised relentings, a father's heartbroken indignation, the trouble of the shepherd over one sheep strayed. His love is manifested even to unrepentant sinners. What is there in the Gospel to lead us to suppose that God will inflict endless and irremediable torments on any whom his love can reach even beyond the grave? Where are we told that the love of God who changes not will be changed into hatred, fury, implacable vengeance, by the moment of death? 'Is it the great crime of dying which can quench the love

[75] *Mercy and Judgement*, p. 444.

that our enmity and our sin could not quench? No! Love never faileth.'[76]

And of course Jesus told us to love our enemies. Will God do less? And if you love someone you don't torture them forever, and you don't annihilate them, destroy them, whether right away or over a long period of time. Love's desire is to build up not knock down, and even more so when we are thinking of agape love.

For human beings to be annihilated or to suffer eternal, everlasting punishment or extinction after a period of punishment would have defeated God's purposes for humanity. It would mean the horror of evil never being finally done away with.

> The question of universalism is usually argued on a basis altogether misleading, i.e. as though the point involved was chiefly, or wholly, man's endless suffering. Odious and repulsive to every moral instinct, as is this dogma, it is not the turning point of this controversy. The vital question is this, that the popular creed by teaching the perpetuity of evil, points to a victorious devil, and to sin as finally triumphant over God. It makes the corrupt, nay the bestial, in our fallen nature to be eternal. It represents what is foulest and most loathsome in man, i.e. the most obstinate sin, as being enduring as God himself. It confers the dignity of immortal life on what is morally abominable. It enthrones pandemonium as an eternal fact, side by side with Paradise; and gazing over its fetid and obscene abysses, is not afraid to call this the triumph of Jesus Christ, this is the realisation of the promises that God shall be 'all in all…'
>
> …With all earnestness, I repeat that our choice lies between accepting the victory of Christ or of evil, and between those alternatives only. Escape from this dilemma there is none… Sin forever present with its taint, even in a single instance, is sin triumphant. Sin, which God has been unable to remove (and has had no resource but to annihilate the sinner) is sin triumphant and death victorious…[77]

Elsewhere Allin writes:

---

[76] Ibid. pp. 445–446.
[77] From *Universalism Asserted*, – Allin, 1895, pp. 285, 287.

The notion of the popular creed, i.e. that God is in the Bible detailing the story of his own defeat, how sin has proved too strong for him, this notion seems wholly unfounded. Assuredly the Bible is not the story of sin, deepening into eternal ruin of God's son, worsted in his utmost effort; it is from opening to close the story of grace stronger than sin – of life victorious over every form of death – of God triumphing over evil.

John Hick also reminds us that extinction also points to the defeat of God's good purposes.

God's good purpose would have failed in the care of all those souls whose fate is extinction. To this extent evil would have prevailed over good and would have permanently marred God's creation.[78]

And he goes on:

…God will eventually succeed in His purpose of winning all men to Himself in faith and love. That this is indeed God's purpose in relation to man is surely evident from the living revelation of that purpose in Jesus Christ. In his life we see at work in our human history – God our saviour, who desires all men to be saved and to come to a knowledge of the truth (1 Timothy 2:3–4).[79]

And an Old Testament verse to run alongside the Timothy passage is Job 42:2: 'No plan of yours can be thwarted.' Now if it is God's will that we be saved, and no plan of his shall be thwarted, then surely this is what will happen.

The accusation comes, are we not then puppets in the hands of God, with no free will. John Hick gives a helpful illustration here,

William James once used the analogy of two chess players, a novice and a world master, to illustrate the compatibility between divine providence and human freedom. Even though the novice is free at every stage to make his own move, we can predict with complete practical certainty that the master will eventually win.

---

[78] *Evil and The God of Love*, 1974 impression, Fontana p. 378.
[79] Ibid. p. 378.

Although we cannot foresee the detailed course of the game, we know that whatever moves the novice makes, the master can respond sooner or later to bring the game to the conclusion that he himself desires.[80]

Hick comments on the fact that as all analogies do, if pressed beyond a certain point they break down. However this I believe is a very helpful analogy indeed. However, Hick goes on to comment (referring to God in relation to the salvation of humanity): 'He is not seeking to subjugate them but to liberate them, in order that they may find in Him their own deepest fulfilment and happiness.'[81]

---

[80] Ibid. p. 380.

[81] Ibid. p. 381, Allin also writes: 'It is said that if a man be not wholly free, his goodness is but a mechanical thing. If so, I reply, better ten thousand fold a mechanical goodness that keeps one at the side of God forever, than a wholly unrestrained freedom which leads to the devil.'

One can also, with the help of a domestic illustration, see love in restricted freedom. There is a large garden, with all kinds of wonderful things in it for the children of the household to enjoy, climb trees, bathe in pools, play games, make decisions, fall and get up again, learn how to care for plants, take delight in nature, learn how to care for the garden, etc. But round this vast garden is a high wall, beyond the wall all kinds of dangers; the mistress of the house knows the children could not handle… the children have absolute freedom of choice within the garden, which may well involve tumbles and hurts, and having to decide what action to take in a host of circumstances, but in love, the freedom is restricted to the garden.

Chapter 8: The Intermediate State

The intermediate state is an essential teaching if we are to have even a glimpse into the problem of suffering in the world for example the undeserved suffering of people who, even taking into consideration the wrongs they have done in life, have to endure an amount of suffering that is out of all proportion to any wrong they have committed.

And if we worship a just God, then surely he knows our thoughts and perplexity when, for example, a person who is kind and considerate to those around them finds themselves tortured by physical pain for years on end, or with mental and emotional agony over loved ones in difficulty, whom they feel helpless to do anything about. And if this kind, considerate person does not believe for very good reasons, because with the best will in the world, they cannot unravel the problem of pain and evil, is this person when they leave this world, when they die, to be then snuffed out like a candle in the dark, annihilated, with no reason or rhyme to what they have seen and endured in life? Or are they to be taken from this mortal life to a life of never-ending misery beyond the grave? Where is justice, if this be the case? However, although all is not answered in the here and now, if we accept the teaching of an intermediate state, where some answers are given, where justice is done, where pilgrimage continues and learning and understanding develop, moving ever nearer to everlasting peace and righteousness – then for us now and for those in the throes of earthly turmoil, there is hope. The Prophet Isaiah, speaking of God's attitude to people, declares, 'A bruised reed he will not break, and a smouldering wick he will not snuff out.' (Isaiah 42:3)

John Austin Baker asks the question:

> Does rejection of God mean a fall into non-being? Or is there some divine equivalent of humanity's judicial penalties, some

pain of alienation from good, which may in time lead the guilty to come to themselves in a far country, and turn back to embrace true retribution: 'treat me like one of your hired servants'? (Luke 15:19). What is certain is that the God who has taken away every human soul into his family will not give up on anyone. In that case a stage of punitive pain, leading, love would hope, to acceptance of redemptive suffering, is more likely than the final writing off implied in annihilation.[82]

This observation of Dr Baker accepts judgement and righteous punishment as part of humanity's pilgrimage, but it is not a hopeless judgement, it is not a judgement without mercy, it is not a punishment without purpose, it is not meaningless retribution. It implies that beyond this earthly scene there is a state before the final summing up of all history, where 'things are put right' and where just punishment is to be meted out. It is remedial, leading to ultimate salvation, so that one gets to the point of recognising one's guilt for wrong words, attitudes, actions, and as did the Prodigal Son, he says, 'I am not worthy to be called your son; make me as one of your hired servants.'[83] And the response of the father, we note, is to embrace the son; he is delighted to welcome him back home. We also notice in this story that although the older son will not come into the house because he is hurt and bitter, the father also goes out to him, and makes it quite clear he wants this son to come in as well, and the father says to him, 'My son, you are always with me, and everything I have is yours. But we had to celebrate and be glad, because this brother of yours was dead and is alive again, he was lost and is found.'[84]

The point Dr Baker is making is the wonderful truth that

---

[82] *The Faith of a Christian*, John Austin Baker, 1996, Dorton, Longman and Todd Ltd, pp. 128–129.

[83] Luke 15:19.

[84] Luke 15:31–32. This parable is told in the context of Pharisees and the teachers of the Law being bitter over the fact that Christ was welcomed 'by sinners'. He was surrounded by them as they crowded round to listen to his teaching (Luke 15:1–2). The Father's desire in this parable to go out to the bitter son tells us he wanted the Pharisees and teachers of the Law to be in his house as well. Christ was bridging the gap between the 'two sons', wanting 'tax collectors, sinners and Pharisees to all be one Family in the Father's house' – as we have already noted, but which needs to be emphasised.

death in unbelief, here, is not the final curtain on our destiny. He makes the point that we all have a part to play in 'perfecting' one another, and he writes:

> For those whom death has robbed of the chance of reconciliation in this life, what joy it will be when each receives our liberated, perfected self as a gift not just from God but also from all those fellow creatures who have been bound up in the bundle of life with us, and whom the Spirit of God has made children in their Father's likeness.[85]

He goes on in a postscript:

> Jesus Christ endured the cross and the grave at human hands, yet still came back with his word of goodwill to be carried to all nations. Because, and only because of that, we know that God's purpose of love towards us is indomitable. He died – the eternal Son of God – so that all of us, Christian or not, could know this for a surety. If he had not died, we could not have known. He died for us all, and that means he died also for me.[86]

It has to be acknowledged, as Dr Austin Baker points out,

> That the traditional picture of judgement is shot through with anomalies and contradictions. First of all, it asks us to believe that God's attitude towards us changes radically the moment we die. While we are in this life, forgiveness and reconciliation are available whenever we are truly sorry and forgive others, but, it would seem, as soon as we die, love and mercy are out. From then on, unrepented serious sin committed in this world excludes us forever from the joy of life in the family of God – and that is the mildest interpretation of 'eternal damnation' or 'punishment'.
>
> For a Christian, such a picture ought to be, in the strict sense of the word, unbelievable. How can it be true that a God who has adopted every human person, regardless of their goodness or badness, as a member of his family, who knows human life from the inside, will suddenly change the whole basis of his relation-

---

[85] *The Faith of a Christian*, p.130. It is of course a truth that God works out his purposes through human beings.
[86] Ibid.

ship with them? He himself would have to become a totally different character. The Israelite prophet knew better, 'for I the Lord do not change; therefore you, O children of Jacob, have not perished'. (Mal 3:6)[87]

Dr Baker also highlights what we have already observed to some degree, but which appears to be ignored by those who hold to a traditionalist view of salvation, namely the situation of those who genuinely can't believe, for one reason or another.

We turn to Dr Baker again:

A somewhat different account of judgement makes it all depend on faith. Those who believe in God and Jesus are safe; those who do not, are lost. In some versions this means specifically believing in the expiation of sin by the death of Jesus on the cross; in others acceptance of the faith of the creeds, or a simple intention to believe what the church believes.

This at once raises the question of all those who have never heard the Gospel, or have never heard it in the form which could commend it. To them we must add the many who have been turned from belief by the confusion and corruption and cruelty of the church, and its insistence on 'tithing mint, dill and cumin' rather than living out 'justice and mercy and faith' (Matt. 23:23).

Then there are the many more who have not been able to reconcile belief in God with intellectual integrity. Surely no honest Christian, one who has struggled with the kind of difficulties for faith that we have been examining, will cast the first stone at them! And if we cannot do that, will the God who vindicated the one who died in God-forsakenness, do so where we refuse?

…How can anyone be judged justly on the basis of their faith and life here, when in this world the evidence of what to believe and how to live is so uncertain? Only when we come into the clear light of the kingdom shall we be in a position to decide, and only then will it be fair to judge us on whatever decision we make.[88]

This approach fits in with 1 Corinthians 13:12 where we read 'Now I know in part; then I shall know fully, even as I am fully known.'

---

[87] Ibid. p. 125.
[88] Ibid. pp. 125–126.

This all points to a state between 'earth and heaven'; that before any final judgement takes place, there is an opportunity to see more clearly beyond the grave and before final entry into that eternal state known as heaven. That one is not plunged immediately into heaven or hell. That there is a place for remedial punishment. That there is a place for appreciating an increasing awareness of truth. That there is a place where we are moulded into what human beings were always meant to be. That there is a place where we understand more and more the beauty of life, where we are able to see more clearly those three which we see reflections of 'here', but 'there' more fully, those which are eternal, that make up the full content of that abundant life of which Jesus Christ spoke: faith, hope and love – the greatest of these being love.

It is of course true that there are those who appear to have a firm clear faith now, who have gained great faith in this life and are sure of their position within their understanding of salvation. But there are still questions that even they will find difficult, and not be able to come to any final conclusions in this life, for example – suffering and justice. But we can be encouraged by the thought that we can begin here; all is not dark here, we do have some light here. Sometimes that light will shine more brightly than at other times, but we can also enter into our present pilgrimage knowing all does not depend on my understanding everything here. But that spiritual exploration, the exploration of the meaning of life, goes on beyond the grave.

For some it is very clear that the biblical position is clearly seen in the direction of an intermediate state. It has been said,

> With educated people it should not be necessary to combat the foolish popular notion that at death men pass into their final destiny – heaven or hell, and then (perhaps thousands of years afterwards) come back to be judged as to final destiny! To state such a belief should be enough to refute it. Those who hold it, do err, not knowing the scriptures.[89]

---

[89] *The Gospel of the Hereafter*, Dr Paterson Smyth, Hodder (no date given) pp. 27–28 (early twentieth century).

The Evangelical Alliance's report touches on the intermediate state on pages 19-20, and encourages a more detailed study of the subject for those 'seeking to relate the traditionalist-conditionalist debate on hell to wider issues of eschatology'. I would like to affirm that a consideration of the intermediate state is crucial to our understanding of eternal destiny, and cannot be divorced from a consideration of the nature of hell.

Some ancient writers have said, as quoted by Paterson Smyth, 'all souls are sequestered in Hades till the day of the Lord' (Turtullian, AD 200).[90] 'Let no man think that souls are judged immediately after death; all are detained in one common place of safe keeping till the time when the supreme judge makes the scrutiny'[91] Lactantius. 'During the interval between death and resurrection, men's souls are kept in hidden receptacles according as they severally deserve rest or punishment' (and in our understanding that punishment would be remedial) Finally Paterson Smyth asks, 'Does it not give a fuller meaning for us to the words of our Lord, 'In my father's house are many mansions (or abiding places)'?[92]

This whole teaching about the intermediate life has been obscured in the Authorised Version of the Bible, where the original word such as Hades has been unfortunately translated 'hell'. Now while it is true that many more people today read up to date versions, and although we have an increasing number of modern translations, the words 'Hades', 'Gehenna' and 'Tartarus' are still sadly translated, 'hell'.

For the Jews of the Lord's time, Hades/Sheol was the place of waiting in the 'unseen'. They also made a distinction within it, the place of the blest, known as 'paradise' or 'Abraham's bosom', or 'under the throne'. The Lord Jesus gives his approval to this belief in the main, using their very own phrases in speaking of the next life; e.g. in the account of Dives and Lazarus, Dives is in Hades (not hell). In the Revised Standard Version we read Lazarus was carried by the angels into Abraham's bosom.[93] And the Lord Jesus

---

[90] Tertullian *De Anima*.
[91] *Div. Instit.*
[92] *Gospel of the Hereafter* p. 31.
[93] Luke 16:22.

on the cross said to the dying criminal, 'Today you shall be with me in paradise.'[94] Jesus did not mean heaven, for he said, 'No man has ascended into heaven, only the Son of Man who is in heaven.'[95] And even Jesus himself did not go directly to Heaven when he died, for he said after his resurrection 'I have not yet ascended to my Father...'[96]

The Bible does point to an intermediate state. Let us now turn to two passages, to which I have already referred, that do just this. In Genesis we read of Abraham's pleading for Sodom, but due to the fact it was so full of unrighteous people, it was destroyed: Genesis 19:27–29. In Ezekiel Chapter 16 we read of its restoration, but these people had been destroyed. Ezekiel 16:53–55 clearly implies that destruction and death in this life does not mean the death of the person, this body being the envelope for life here – the 'person' moves on.[97]

In 1 Peter 3:18 to 4:6, we read:

> Christ himself died once and for all for sins. The upright for the sake of the guilty, to lead us to God. In the body he was put to death, in the spirit he was raised to life, and, in the spirit, he went to preach to the spirits in prison.

This is why the Gospel was brought to the dead as well, so that, though in their bodies they had undergone the judgement that faces humanity, in their spirit they might enjoy the life of God.

As has been noted before those who believe in no intermediate state, and advocate eternal punishment or annihilation after death, before judgement or after, have sometimes accused those who do not hold their views of 'explaining away texts' which appear to them to bolster their position; but it is equally true that they do

---

[94] Luke 23:43.

[95] John 3:13.

[96] John 20:17.

[97] Jesus came back to the disciples with a new kind of body, not limited to time or space, yet undoubtedly the same person, for the wounds of the cross were still upon him. In Colossians we read of Jesus as being 'the first born from among the dead', Colossians 1:18. The first to have this kind of resurrection body, physical yet spiritual, not a ghost, as Jesus was at pains to point out in the Gospel accounts, was recognisably the Jesus of Nazareth they knew.

the same with texts which do not support their stance. Take the passages we have looked at, for example it would appear the truth lies in looking at the whole Bible to see where the general ethos lies. I maintain it points to an intermediate state, to an opportunity beyond this body to respond to the good news, and that God's will will not be thwarted; his will will be done on earth as in Heaven. The universe will be saved, the whole created order.

The Bible is clear that there is judgement, there is punishment for wrongdoing, but there is mercy. When the sentence has been carried out, the punishment administered for wrongdoing, then comes salvation. Punishment and destruction does not have the last word. Here I emphasise what has already been alluded to. Christ himself preached to the 'dead' who in the days of Noah had refused to listen to God – the vast majority, in fact – so what does the good shepherd do? He does what you would expect him to do. The good shepherd in his search goes even beyond the grave for the lost to bring them the good news, the gospel; death is not a barrier to him.[98]

Nigel Wright, a self-confessed evangelical, writes:

> The key question, therefore, is not so much whether human beings can be redeemed beyond death, as whether God's search for his fallen creatures is thwarted by death or continues beyond it. The judge of all the earth will certainly do right, but from the perspective we currently occupy, it is reasonable to suppose that this includes a universal search to win human beings to relationship with himself which does not cease at the point of human death.[99]

David Edwards draws our attention to some of the most significant theologians of the church who espoused the wider hope, that response to Christ is not limited to this present earthly life:

---

[98] Surely one should be very cautious indeed to advocate eternal punishment, annihilation, and only one opportunity to respond in the present life, when there are passages such as I have referred to, even if they were the only indication, because of the great danger to the emotions and minds of even some, by the horrors of the 'one opportunity and eternal punishment' teaching.

[99] Nigel Wright, *The Radical Evangelical*, SPCK, 1996, p. 99.

...Origen, Maurice, Schleiermacher, Barth – what a row of theological giants! And all universalists have been in very good company in believing that this is in the purpose of God. They have also been thoroughly in accordance with hopes expressed in the New Testament itself when they have hoped that after death God's goodness, as declared in Christ, will appeal to those who did not accept the Gospel of Christ while alive on earth. In the New Testament as well as in these universalist theologians, the hope is clear and strong that this activity of God's goodness after death will heal mankind... St John the Divine, in his vision of the final city of God, saw two trees of life 'the leaves of the trees serve for the healing of the nations, and every accursed thing shall disappear' (Rev. 22).[100]

David Edwards allows for this wider hope, while including the possibility that some will say no to God here in this present state and beyond the grave, then 'God may take man's "no" for an answer'.[101] In this connection I would draw attention to Jurgen Moltmann when he comments on 'Man's free will':

The logic of hell seems to me not merely inhumane but also extremely atheistic: here the human being in his freedom of choice is his own lord and god. His own will is his heaven – or his hell. God is merely the accessory who puts that will into effect. If I decide for heaven, God must put me there; if I decide for hell, he has to leave me there. If God has to abide by our free decision, then we can do with him what we like. Is that 'the love of God'? Free human beings forge their own happiness and are their own executioners. They do not just dispose over their lives here; they decide on their eternal destinies as well. So they have no need of any God at all. After a God has perhaps created us free as we are, he leaves us to our fate. Carried to this ultimate conclusion, the logic of hell is secular humanism, as Feuerbach, Marx and Nietzsche already perceived a long time ago.[102]

Taking this on board and as we have already seen God will not take mans 'no' for an answer but continues to woo humanity to a

---

[100] David Edwards, *The Last Things Now*, SCM, 1969, pp. 77–78.
[101] Ibid.
[102] As quoted in *The Eschatology of Jurgen Moltmann*, ed. R Bauckham, T & T Clark 1999, p. 45.

realisation of his salvation. And Martin Luther, the great Reformer, has written: 'God forbid that I should limit the time for acquiring faith to the present life; in the depths of the divine mercy there may be opportunity to win it in the future state.'[103]

The love of God, from what we have observed thus far, sees us through this life and beyond the grave – his love is not thwarted by death. Like the good shepherd in Luke 15 he seeks and goes on seeking the lost sheep till he finds it. This is the love of God in Christ, this is the foundation of salvation, not our faith, not our works, but his love, his desire to see us all saved, to be brought back to our spiritual roots – it is to this foundation of salvation we shall now turn.

[103] Letter to Hansen von Rechenburg, 1523, quoted by F W Farrar in *Mercy and Judgement*, MacMillan 1881, p.24.

Chapter 9: Comment on the Foundation of Salvation

What the Evangelical Alliance's Report fails to grasp, it seems to me, is the supreme importance of agape love. Salvation comes first and foremost through this grace of love, undeserved favour toward us. This love which produces such grace is greater than faith, as is clearly spelt out in 1 Corinthians 13:13: 'Meanwhile these three remain, faith, hope and love; but the greatest of these is love.' This is where the foundation of salvation lies personally and cosmically.

The Report is in danger of becoming Pharisaic in that it would limit salvation to certain rigid rules, the rule of salvation through faith alone, with their own particular understanding of 'faith'. This implies a limited salvation, just as the Pharisees in Christ's day would limit salvation to just one race of people, the Jewish nation, when in Christ we are all one human family.[104]

When we understand that agape comes before all else in salvation, then faith, trust in genuine selfless love is the basis, so that it is not so much 'grace through faith', but 'faith through grace'. It has to be this way if love from which grace springs is the one value over and above all else, and it is through this love that true justice springs.

Love takes into account conditions which a rule may not cover, and it takes changing circumstances into consideration. Rules of law are rigid and can lead to bondage, this is why Jesus summed up the Law in love: 'Love God, love your neighbour, this fulfils the Law.'[105] How do we know that we love God? By loving our neighbour, and we come full circle. As it says in 1 John: 'How can you love God who you cannot see, if you do not love your brother who you can see?'[106]

---

[104] 'Here is no Greek or Jew, circumcised or uncircumcised, Barbarian, Scythian, slave or free.' 1 Cor.
[105] Matthew 22:37–40.
[106] 1 John 4:19–21.

Jesus deliberately goes against the Law God gave to the Israelites in the Old Testament – 'an eye for an eye, and a tooth for a tooth'.[107] Instead he says, 'But I tell you; do not take revenge on someone who does you wrong…'[108]

But he makes it clear he comes to fulfil the Law (Matthew 5:17–18) Not the smallest letter, not the least stroke of the pen, will by any means disappear from the Law until everything is accomplished. Jesus came to fulfil laws. How does he then fulfil them if, as we have seen, he breaks them – as in the case of an eye for an eye, a tooth for a tooth?

The only explanation that I believe is open to us is that Jesus understands the Law as being summed up by love – all the Law and the prophets, all the smallest details are summed up by love.

Jesus Christ fulfilled the Law when on the cross he said, 'Father, forgive them, they know not what they do.' (Luke 23:34) He forgives them, even when they are not asking forgiveness for themselves (I believe this to be a valid understanding of the text). This is love beyond the letter of the Law. Paul writes:

'We have been released from the Law so that we serve in the new way of the spirit, and not in the old way of the written code.'[109] And in the letter to the Corinthians he writes: 'He has made us competent as ministers of a new covenant – not of the letter but of the spirit; for the letter kills, but the spirit gives life.'[110] Then he goes on to say how much more glorious this is. It is the spirit of the Law which follows the way of love. James in his letter describes this special agape love as the 'royal Law'. He, no doubt, has in mind the way Jesus sums up all the Law and the prophets with 'love God, love your neighbour'. Love's the foundation for salvation received and lived. It is this love which fulfils the written and oral Law in the smallest detail. Jesus fulfilled it completely; we are called to learn this way.

Thus we can say that even the doctrinal Law as set out in the Evangelical Alliance's Report ('we would underline here that from a biblical viewpoint, however widely God's salvation extends, it is

---

[107] Exodus 21:24; Leviticus 24:20, Deuteronomy 19:21.
[108] Matthew 5:39, *The Living Bible*.
[109] Romans 7:6.
[110] 2 Corinthians 3:6.

salvation which comes by grace through faith, rather than by right')[111] limits the grace of God to faith which, according to scripture, is subordinate to love. It is true that salvation comes to us 'not by right', for it is of grace, which springs from agape love; but it is not our faith or even our love but his love for us which gives salvation. The basis for salvation is this:

'This is love, not that we loved God, but that He loved us, and sent his son as an atoning sacrifice for our sins. Dear friends, since God so love us, we ought to love one another.'[112] And we read in the letter to the Romans: 'God demonstrates his love for us in this: while we were still sinners, Christ died for us.'[113]

We have been justified through faith, but this is not the ultimate means to salvation, which is love, a love that will stand by us even with our doubts and lack of faith. We are of course not justified by our works any more than by our faith, or our love, but it is his love for us, his faithfulness towards us that saves us. Our acts of love, works of love, expressions of faithfulness, are the result of his love in us, working out through us. For our love, faith and good works would never reach high enough – but his love, his faithfulness will see us through, and wherever his kind of love is expressed, this is a response to him, from whatever culture or religion, and in the fullness of time whether in this life or in the life beyond, the source of that love will ultimately be recognised, 'if it is God's will that all be saved',[114] which is what the scriptures say.

So if it is God's will that all be saved, all will be saved, even beyond the 'norm', the set rule of salvation (if we can call it that), for Job informs us 'his plan cannot be thwarted.'[115] His love will not let man's will ultimately triumph over his will; he will woo humanity until his love is responded to.

For grace which springs from his love fulfils all laws, by going beyond them. This is what Jesus did.

So I would submit that a conservative evangelical basis for

---

[111] Evangelical Alliance Report p. 35.
[112] 1 John 4:10–11.
[113] Romans 5:8.
[114] 2 Peter 3:9.
[115] Job 42:2.

salvation is in danger of, if not actually committing the mistake of the Pharisees and teachers of the Law, of Christ's day, in saying that if you fail to comply with the formula 'by faith alone', then you are lost.[116] The formula can become a rule, where the letter rather than the spirit is all important, when in fact the Gospel has come to set us free to love, as Christ loves; to aspire to this which enhances all loves and leads to a true righteousness. This is good news, it is the good news of a wider hope, in Christ. It is his love that saves us.

This love takes into consideration the heart of the human being. Love cannot be straightjacketed into any watertight formula. While we have to have rules in life, 'laws', as a general principle, these however cannot have the final word in all circumstances. Agape will bring love to the undeserving, love when love is not returned. To love like this even when one is unaware of the source is salvation, and we come back to the cross with the words of forgiveness on Christ's lips, we return to Matthew 25, when it is certainly implied that those who were giving water to the thirsty, food to the hungry, giving hospitality to the stranger, clothes to the naked, succour to the sick, visiting the prisoner, in other words caring for the destitute, were serving Christ himself, though they did not know it! It was Christ's kind of love working through them, and his love was the foundation of their salvation.

The importance of the concept of God as the spirit which is love (which one would wish to explore further) has crucial implications for living practical Christianity. Even in the midst of our questions we can still learn to express the kind of love Christ manifested on the cross which cuts the cycle of revenge and the propagation of bitterness and hate. Christ on the cross did not allow the attitude of those who had him crucified to dictate his attitude to them. His was one of compassionate love. Even while he felt forsaken and did not understand why he was forsaken by God and man, crying out, 'My God, my God, why have you forsaken me?' (Matthew 27:46), his love still operated.

---

[116] By saying 'by faith alone', you are relying on your faith as a rule for being saved, rather than God's love for you in Christ.

In closing I would wish to draw attention to Romans 4, which is the basis for justification by faith according to Protestant theology. In that chapter we notice faith came for Abraham before the rules came. In this case it was the rule of circumcision – he received the blessings because he trusted in God's promises; he was not trusting in himself, and indeed he would have to have reminders of God's promises, and he would fail in his faith,[117] but despite his unworthiness, he would receive the promises, because God loved him, and because God's will would be done in spite of all the obstacles against it.

Even when the promises are forgotten or not trusted or believed, one can still be saved because God keeps his promises – this is love, this is grace, undeserved favour toward us, and is all from a sovereign God. The crucial urgency is for this love to be expressed in our present world; to turn people from all that would destroy life to all that gives life, now and always – the compassionate wisdom of eternal love (agape).

As we have already noted, when the disciples lost faith, forgot Christ's promises to them, or failed to trust in them, when they were huddled together numbed by the horror of it all – the cross, the suffering, the loss of hope in the face of death, the death of one they loved and had pinned all their hopes on – Jesus came to them as the resurrected Christ, and gave them back their faith and hope with his word of love (we may feel we have no hope, no faith, but in and through the love of Jesus the facts are very different). Jesus said, 'Peace be with you!' (John 20:20) He repeats it to them and to Thomas, who was not with them when Jesus came to them; Jesus then makes a visit to Thomas, who still could not believe, and repeats his message of reassurance. Jesus believed in them even when they could not believe in him. A message for all those who can and can't believe, the message of love: 'Now these three remain: faith, hope and love, but the greatest of these is love.'

This is our salvation! For past, present and future!

---

[117] Genesis 12:10–13. His faith in God failed in Egypt for fear the Egyptians would kill him for his wife, so he told his wife to tell them she was his sister.

APPENDIX

WIDER HOPE from the HISTORY of FAITH

EUSEBIUS of GAUL, +371 – Speaking of 'those worthy of temporal punishment', and referring to Matthew v.26, he says, 'In proportion to the matter of the sin will be the lingering in the passage. In proportion to the growth of the fault will be the discipline of the discerning flame; in proportion to the things which iniquity in its folly hath wrought will be the severity of the wise punishment.' – De Epiph. Hom. iii.

ST ANSELM, +1109 – 'It is not just that God should altogether suffer to perish His creature which He hath made.'

'God demands from no sinner more than he owes; but since no one can pay as much as he owes, Christ alone paid for all more than the debt due.'

MARTIN LUTHER, +1546 – 'God forbid that I should limit the time for acquiring faith to the present life. In the depths of the divine mercy there may be opportunity to win it in the future state.' – Letter to Hansen von Rechenberg, 1523. (Luther's Briefe, ii. 454.)

BISHOP JEREMY TAYLOR, +1667 – 'It is a strange consideration to suppose an eternal torment to those to whom it was never threatened, to those who never heard of Christ... to people surprised in a single crime, to those that die young in their natural follies and foolish lusts, to them that in a sudden gaiety and excessive joy, to all alike; to all infinite and eternal, even to unwarned people; and that this should be inflicted by God, who infinitely loves His creatures, who died for them, who pardons easily, and pities readily, and excuses much, and delights in our being saved, and would not have us die...'

'It is certain that God's mercies are infinite, and it is also certain that the matter of eternal torments cannot truly be understood; and when the schoolmen go about to reconcile the divine justice to that severity, and consider why God punishes eternally a temporal sin or a state of evil, they speak variously and uncertainly and unsatisfyingly.' – Sermon on Christ's Advent to Judgment. (Works, iv. 43.)

CANON CHARLES KINGSLEY, +1875 – 'Can these dark dogmas be true of a Father who bids us be perfect as He is, in that He sends His sun to shine on the evil and the good, and His rain on the just and unjust? Or of a Son who so loved the world that He died to save the world, – and surely not in vain?

'These questions... educated men and women of all classes and denominations – orthodox, be it remembered, as well as unorthodox – are asking, and will ask more and more until they receive an answer. And if we of the clergy cannot give them an answer which accords with their conscience and reason, if we tell them that the words of Scripture and the integral doctrines of Christianity demand the same notions of moral retribution as were current in the days when men racked criminals, burned heretics alive, and believed that every Mussulman whom they slaughtered in a crusade went straight to endless torments, – then evil times will come both for the clergy and the Christian religion for many a year henceforth.' – Water of Life, p.71.

DR WHITE, +1712 Fellow of Trinity College, Cambridge, Preacher to the Council of State, Domestic Chaplain to Oliver Cromwell.

'As sin and death were not brought in at first, so it is certain that they shall not be the end; for grace is the beginning of all, and the end must be grace also.' – Restitution of All Things, p. 245.

SIR ISAAC NEWTON, +1723 – 'The degree and the duration of the torments of these degenerate and anti-Christian people should be no other than that which would be approved of by those angels who had ever laboured for their salvation, and that Lamb who had redeemed them with His most precious blood.' – On Rev. xiv. 10,11.

DR ISAAC WATTS, +1748 – 'There is not one place of Scripture where the word "death", as it was first threatened in the law of innocency, necessarily signifies a certain miserable immortality of the soul either of Adam, the actual sinner, or to his posterity.' – The Ruin and Decay of Mankind, Question xi.

DR SAMUEL JOHNSON, +1784 – 'The generality of

mankind are neither so obstinately wicked as to deserve everlasting punishment, nor so good as to merit being admitted into the society of the blessed spirits; and God is therefore graciously pleased to allow a middle state, where they may be purified by a certain degree of suffering.'... 'Some of the texts of Scripture on these subjects are, as you observe, indeed strong, but they may admit of a mitigated interpretation.'

FRIEDRICH SCHLEIERMACHER, +1834 – 'Through the force of the Redemption a universal restoration of souls will follow.' – Glaubenslehre, # 163.

BIBLIOGRAPHY

Allin, T, *Universalism Asserted*, William & Norgate, 1885.

Baker, John Austin, *The Faith of a Christian*, Darton, Longman & Todd, 1996.

Bonda, Jan, *The One Purpose of God*, Eerdmans, 1998.

Craig, Mary, *Candles in the Dark*, Hodder & Stoughton, 1993.

Cassidy, Sheila, *Introducing Good Friday People*, Darton, Longman & Todd, 1991.

Dixon, Larry, *The Other Side of Good News*, (Victor) Bridge Point, 1992.

Edwards, David, *After Death?*, Continuum, 1999.

—— *The Last Things Now*, SCM, 1969.

Farrar, F W, *Mercy and Judgment*, McMillan, 1881.

Hick, John, *Evil and the God of Love*, Collins, 1974.

Israel, Martin, *Life Eternal*, SPCK, 1992.

Klassen, Randolph, *What does the Bible really say about hell?*, Pandora Press 2001.

Kenneth, Brother Kenneth, *Saints of the 20th Century*, Mowbrays, 1976.

Massadie, Gerald, *The History of the Devil*, New Leaf, Boxtree, 1996.

Milne, Bruce, from *Preaching the Word*, addresses from the Evangelical Assembly, Christian Focus, 2004.

Morgan, Chris, *Jonathan Edwards & Hell*, Mentor, 2004.

Moltmann, Jurgen, 'The Logic of Hell' in *The Eschatology of Jurgen Moltman*, R Bauckham [ed.], T & T Clark, 1999.

Oppenheimer, Helen, *The Hope of Heaven*, Cowley Publications, 1988.

Priestland, Gerald, *Priestland's Progress*, BBC, 1981.

Polkinghorne, John, *The God of Hope and the End of the World*, SPCK, 2002.

Sykes, William, *Visions of Love*, Bible Reading Fellowship, 1992.

Smyth, Paterson, *The Gospel of the Hereafter*, Hodder.

Wallace, Stuart (ed), *Does God Exist?*, Ashgate Publishing, 2003.

Westcott, B F, *Revelation of the Father*, MacMillan, 1887.

Wright, Nigel, *The Radical Evangelical*, SPCK, 1996.

'The Nature of Hell', report by the Evangelical Alliance, Acute, 2000.

Printed in the United Kingdom
by Lightning Source UK Ltd.
115788UKS00001B/73